SIXTY
SOMETHINGS

SIXTY
SOMETHINGS

The lives of women who remember the Sixties

NICOLA MADGE & PAUL HOGGART

with illustrations by Geo Parkin

QUARTET BOOKS

First published in 2020 by Quartet Books Limited
A member of the Namara Group
27 Goodge Street, London, W1T 2LD

Copyright © Nicola Madge and Paul Hoggart 2020

The moral right of the author has been asserted by them in accordance with the Copyright, Designs and Patents Act, 1988

All rights reserved.
No part of this publication may be reproduced, stored in a retrieval system, or transmitted in any form or by any means, without the prior permission in writing of the publisher, nor be otherwise circulated in any form of binding or cover other than that in which it is published and without a similar condition including this condition being imposed on the subsequent purchaser

Reasonable efforts have been made to find the copyright holders of third party copyright material. An appropriate acknowledgement can be inserted by the publisher in any subsequent printing or edition

A catalogue record for this book is available from the British Library

ISBN 9780704374744

Typeset by Tetragon, London
Printed and bound in Great Britain by
TJ International Ltd, Padstow, Cornwall

Beneath every history, another history.
HILARY MANTEL

Where you grew up becomes a big part of who you are for the rest of your life. You can't run away from that. Well, sometimes the running away from it is what makes you who you are.
HELEN MIRREN

The sixties were a time when ordinary people could do extraordinary things . . . !
TWIGGY

I have grown up but that should be a positive thing. When you look at a photo album it's lovely to remember being so young but it's also good to know you grew up!
JENNY AGUTTER

Youth is not everything. Now we have all the baby boomers in their sixties, like me, who are actively engaged in life – we're not retiring, we're not just being put out to grass once we hit sixty.
JULIE WALTERS

What will you do now with the gift of your left life?
CAROL ANN DUFFY

ACKNOWLEDGEMENTS

Our purpose in writing *Sixty Somethings* is to provide an account of the lives of a group of women, born after the end of the Second World War and living through the Sixties, from their earliest memories to the present. We are therefore indebted to *our* Sixty Somethings for volunteering their stories and submitting themselves to our endless questions in such good spirit. Without them there would be no book. They were not only enormously informative, but also greatly entertaining. We hope we have done justice to their experiences and that they are pleased with the story that has emerged.

While we ourselves are totally responsible for the content of the book, we are most grateful to those who helped to get it to the point of publication. Very many thanks here go to Rosemary Gray, sister of one of our Sixty Somethings, who directed us towards publishers we might approach. Once in conversation with Quartet Books, we were delighted when Naim Attallah offered us a contract. We also appreciated the tremendous encouragement and support we received from David Elliott, who showed great faith in the book from the start. Further down the line, Peter Jacobs was incredibly friendly, helpful and efficient in turning the manuscript into a book, while Georgia de Chamberet greatly assisted on the marketing and publicity side. There were many other unidentified people who contributed to the process, and we would like to give our thanks to them as well.

The lives recounted throughout this book had their ups and downs, their joys and their sadnesses. What was remarkable, however, was how our Sixty Somethings were quick to see the funny side of much that had happened, even if only in hindsight. The amazing illustrations by Geo Parkin bring out some of this humour, and we are incredibly lucky that he was able to produce so many amusing drawings despite a tight schedule.

We would be remiss if we did not also recognise the support and encouragement of our families and friends, whether by regaling us with questions on the project's progress, acting as a sounding board for our ideas, or just watching on the sidelines. Thank you.

CONTENTS

1. Setting the Scene — 11
2. An Inheritance: Grandparents and Parents — 21
3. Growing Up — 61
4. Talking About My Generation — 97
5. The Adult Years — 136
6. When I'm Sixty-Four… — 177
7. How's It All Turned Out? — 217

I

Setting the Scene

The 'Swinging Sixties' are commonly depicted as hedonistic days. A point in history remembered for the generation of young people who shed the trappings of their parents and grandparents and, fuelled by sex, drugs and rock 'n' roll, set out to put the world to rights. A time when individuality was heralded and convention widely challenged. A time without precedent.

But what was it really like and what is that generation up to now? Is sixty really the new forty? The two writers had, before embarking on this project, been impressed by how many of their contemporaries, now in their sixties and above, seemed to be as active, youthful and eager for new experiences as they had been in their forties, thirties and, in some cases, even their twenties. Despite pursuing careers, raising families, many becoming grandparents, some caring for ageing parents or enduring all manner of medical problems, these new hipsters, some literally with new hips, seemed to have an undiminished appetite for life.

This book looks back over the lives of 67 Sixty Something women who lived through the Sixties to explore these questions. What did they expect from their lives, and were they so different from those of their parents and grandparents and, indeed, even their children? Had their youthful ideals and expectations been matched by reality? Many university-educated women in the sixties grew up with left-of-centre political beliefs but are now living in a Western world where right-wing tendencies are taking ever greater hold. And what was it like getting older? Were these women feeling their age in the autumn of their lives, or was there still life in them yet?

These women had been born shortly after the end of the Second World War at a time of optimism. Peace had come even if it had come at a price. For several years rationing remained severe and there were all sorts of shortages. British towns and cities were pockmarked with bomb sites. But there were hopes of better times ahead. The men were back from fighting, welfare reforms were in progress, rationing would gradually come to an end and the country was beginning to rebuild itself. The sudden peak in the birth rate at this time was perhaps a symbolic reflection of the wish to look forward rather than back.

Indeed, the number of new babies was remarkable. The birth rate in England and Wales had fallen to an all-time low of 579,091 in 1941, the year after a record number of deaths, but then increased, with a slight dip in 1945, to a peak of 881,026 in 1947. It declined and steadied after this time before going up again in the second half of the 1950s and reaching a second peak in the mid-1960s. There was a notable decline thereafter, probably in part due to the introduction of the Abortion Act in 1967.

This new optimism came to characterise the new generation. It was a 'golden age', said Frances. 'We were freed from older patterns of thought.' After the disruption of the war, youngsters wanted to change the world, added Clara. They also felt they could do whatever they wished. According to Jacca, 'My life was not defined for me in any shape or form … If I wanted to go to the moon, I could do it.' They believed in peace and love and expected everything to get better and better, not only for themselves but also for their children and grandchildren. 'I always believed that things were going to get better financially,' said Theresa. As Miranda said, there was a new wave of hope and way of running the country and, according to Lilian, they were not going to be like their parents. They would do things differently, live life to the full and (maybe) never become old.

Because of their numbers and their lifestyle, members of the generation in question are often referred to in the media and elsewhere as 'Baby Boomers', a term some objected to in no uncertain terms. These so-called 'Baby Boomers' are both admired and despised, credited with bringing about enormous social progress but blamed for all manner of sociopolitical ills. Some have seen them as pioneers of a new kind of enlightenment, especially in matters of sexual politics, in openness and honesty about emotional matters and in their readiness to challenge authority. Others have deplored what they see as their rampant self-indulgence, economic irresponsibility and lack of respect for traditional moral values. Living through a period of rapid social change, they are now often heralded – fairly or unfairly – as 'lucky', 'privileged' or even greedy and unscrupulous in holding on to wealth and jobs and disadvantaging younger generations. 'Baby Boomers' have attracted considerable attention in all these ways and, as Hazel Grace said, the media construct of a Baby Boomer is a kind of hate figure, 'something you identify with and loathe at the same time'. How did they react to being lumbered with this label?

There has been much written about Sixty Somethings, detailing their childhoods, their lives during the sixties, or their interpretations of 'older age', but a paucity of studies of their thoughts and experiences over their entire lifespan. What is presented here is not such a study but rather a rich account of the lives of a particular set of such women.

The Sixty Somethings

The women whose experiences are recounted throughout this book all volunteered to take part. The main requisites for participation were that they were born after the end of the Second World War and were at least sixty at the time of interview. They were also required to be or have become middle class, although this was not strictly defined. A few of the women were friends and other contacts of the authors, but the rest were found through snowballing and from invitations to take part sent out via various channels.

The women were distributed across the age band as a whole, with more at the older end than the younger. Of the 67, 28 were born from 1945 to 1949, 29 from 1950 to 1954 and 10 from 1955 to 1958. The greatest number of women to be born in a single year was 10, in 1951.

Many women had moved geographically over their lives, and where they were born was not necessarily where they were living at the time of interview. The London region was the most common place for the women to have both been born and to be living. This was followed by the South East, East Anglia and the North West for place of birth, and by the South West, the South East, Yorkshire and Humberside and Scotland for current place of abode. Wales, the North East and Northern Ireland were the least represented regions of the UK.

From what they told us, 34 women were currently married, five were widowed without partners, and 12 were single and living alone. Ten were cohabiting and the remaining five had partners but did not live with them.

These 67 women are certainly not representative of their birth cohort, as they themselves repeatedly pointed out. They are women who largely consider themselves 'lucky' or 'privileged' – although not without caveat. Not all have come from middle-class backgrounds, even if this is where they are now. They are aware that they are talking about their own lives and that their wider world views are coloured by their middle-class point of view, their education, their ability to take advantage of the welfare state, their financial achievements, where they grew up and, quite simply, their own experiences. 'I live in a little bubble,' explained Elizabeth. Moreover, they were aware of the difficulties of generalising from their own case and often pointed to neighbours, friends and siblings with very different childhoods and life stories. They recognised that the advantages they had had probably applied only, according to Annie, to a small strata of people. Even among themselves there were enormous differences. 'In a way we've been typecast,' said Primrose, 'but we're very very varied.'

Gathering the women's stories

Most women told their stories through telephone interviews held with one or other of the two authors, a small number of others in face-to-face interviews. All were asked to choose a reference name, and most selected pseudonyms. These names are used in the comments and quotes reported throughout the book. Names are, however, omitted where there is particularly sensitive information that could lead to identification, particularly if this includes reference to somebody other than the woman herself.

The female author meets the criteria for Sixty Somethings and, while not one of the 67 women, has (under pseudonym) occasionally contributed her own experiences to the discussion. The male author's sister, who also meets the criteria, has also made occasional contributions, again under a pseudonym.

The rest of the book

The women's lives are retold from their own perspectives throughout the rest of the book. Chapter Two begins with the Sixty Somethings recalling their memories and impressions of grandparents and parents to set the scene and provide the social and historical context into which they were born. Most had known either one or two grandparents to some degree, and these were variously remembered as affectionate or distant and strict. Lives were sometimes tough and characterised by poverty and austerity, but at other times more comfortable even if still fairly simple and frugal. Attitudes to marriage and illegitimacy had been far more prescribed than in their own generation, but there were still stories of scandal and mystique to be passed on and told. Conditions improved for the next generation, the Sixty Somethings' own parents, partly due to better education and opportunities for social advancement, especially among fathers. However, the onset of World War I interrupted lives in both generations, bringing with it hardship and loss. At the same time, nonetheless, it provided many women with opportunities for rewarding work and, for some, brought excitement. Its end also heralded a new age and a significant population boom.

Chapter Three begins the chronological story of the Sixty Somethings' lives. Born during this boom and within a few years of the end of the war, many experienced austerity that gradually gave way to greater prosperity and comfort rather than extravagance. The great majority of the women were brought up by two married parents, typically with one or two siblings, in households where traditional family roles prevailed. Fathers generally worked while mothers gave up any jobs they may have had to remain at home with their small children. The Sixty Somethings spoke variously about their relationships with parents, but commonly observed a greater distance, both emotionally and in openness about topics such as sex, between them than they'd subsequently experienced with their own children. Despite fairly rigid discipline in some families, the young Sixty Somethings were nonetheless still allowed a lot of unsupervised freedom in their localities. Schooling was an important aspect of their lives, acclaimed by many, that paved the way for larger numbers to go to university than in earlier times. Parents differed in their attitudes to their daughters' futures, some holding to traditional roles for women and others wishing to see them have the opportunities they had themselves been denied.

Most of the Sixty Somethings went to university or some form of higher education during their lives, usually upon leaving school. Chapter Four charts their reactions to breaking away from their families and their experiences of the sex, drugs and rock 'n' roll often attributed to them. While some embraced the Swinging Sixties with a vengeance, others were notable bystanders, perhaps affected by the mood of the generation even if not fully-fledged participants. This mood, generated in part by new opportunities after the war, a sense of liberation, intellectual debate and a growing welfare state, led to new forms of culture and counterculture largely specific to the generation. There also seemed to be a strong belief in anti-conformity, even if this was often in fact conformity to new norms, and active protest against injustice. The relationship between the sexes, and a rising interest in feminism and gender equality, were debated passionately by many at this time.

Chapter Five moves on to examine the adult years of the Sixty Somethings, or at least the period in which they settled, or didn't settle, into building families and careers. Most of the women had married at some point or had other long-term commitments, with more than one in three experiencing marital breakdown. Eight in ten were parents. Compared to their parents, they were more likely to have multiple partners and get divorced, and more likely to think they had close and open relationships with their children. More, compared to their mothers, also worked. It was easy to find employment and many of the Sixty Somethings were well qualified. Although, like their mothers, they may have given up work while their children were young, they were much more likely to have found a job again later. Despite a bias towards teaching, followed by health and welfare, a number of women worked in male-dominated occupations. Overall, two in three believed they had remained in approximately the same social class as their parents.

Earning their own money, and being able to administer their own financial affairs, had not generally been the experience of women in earlier generations.

Chapter Six explores the women's lives at the time of interview, in their sixties or early seventies. With increasing life expectancy, and in good health despite a few extra aches and pains, most had many years ahead to look forward to. Although a few were still in paid employment, the majority were actively embracing a new phase in their life, participating in voluntary activities, going on holidays, looking after grandchildren and sometimes elderly parents, learning new things, keeping themselves fit and healthy, or doing things they'd always wanted to do but hadn't previously had time for. Sex was still in evidence, and drinking a bit too much wine seemed to be the most common weakness. Most Sixty Somethings didn't like to think of themselves as 'old', stressing that this was not how they felt. Reluctantly, however, they accepted they were getting older, many hoping to be at least a bit disgraceful along the way. Losing independence and becoming a burden were particularly dreaded.

In the final Chapter Seven, the women reflect on how everything has turned out. Almost all reiterated how lucky they had been to have been born when they had. They had been better off and had more opportunities than their parents, their education had been good, there had been plenty of jobs for them, and most were now comfortably off, with homes they owned and pensions from work. Things were looking decidedly bleaker for their children, whose chances of home ownership and generous pensions seemed much slimmer. Despite being a fortunate generation, however, they were adamant that they did not deserve the resentment they often encountered. Many argued how they had campaigned for a fairer society, worked hard and done what they could for a better future, and that their good fortune was not directly of their making. They had just been lucky.

But there were disappointments too. Many Sixty Somethings were very unhappy at the direction in which twenty-first century society seemed to be going. Their generation had perhaps helped to usher in a greater tolerance of diversity and individuality alongside a lesser tolerance of social injustice and disrespect, but much of the progress many of them pioneered seemed to have gone into remission. Inequality in society, for instance, had not gone away. The Sixty Somethings might be the lucky ones, but there were millions of people in their generation who had not been as fortunate. Class still makes a massive difference in Britain, as does where people live and the chances life presents them with. Almost all the women were very keen to make this point. Emphatically.

2

An Inheritance: Grandparents and Parents

The first half of the twentieth century, when the grandparents and parents of the Sixty Somethings were growing up and leading adult lives, saw massive, if gradual, changes in everyday life. This period saw the arrival of the cinema, the 'wireless' radio, telephones and television. Motor transport gradually replaced horse-drawn vehicles, while the first fragile biplanes appeared, to be superseded eventually by jet airliners. Domestic chores were gradually made less arduous by electrical labour-saving devices. Important social changes were in progress too, with rising living standards, extended education, a changing profile of employment opportunities, the growing emancipation of women, a widening of pension provision and advances in public health. Life was generally much harder for the Sixty Somethings' grandparents, even those with middle-class occupations, than for their parents.

It was not all about progress, however. There were also the transformative disruptions of two world wars and all they brought in their wake. All grandparents and parents had lived through at least one of these, in marked contrast to the Sixty Somethings, and in most cases the impact was profound. Their experiences during these times, as well as their own personal legacies, were without doubt often key influences on the formative years of the Sixty Somethings themselves. They provided both a backdrop and a point of comparison.

Memories of grandparents

Most Sixty Somethings had memories or knowledge of their grandparents, although six had never had any direct contact with them. Even when they had met, the women's direct interaction with grandparents varied enormously, depending on how long the grandparents had survived after the women were born.

Life expectancy was indeed dramatically lower around the time when the grandparents were likely to have been born than in later years and generations. Around 1900, for example, average life expectancy was about 47 for a man and 50 for a woman. Nonetheless, many people survived beyond this age, as the statistics reflect the large numbers of people dying in childhood. From then onwards, however, social conditions improved, along with average life expectancy. Most people had better diets, there were improvements in public health – reflected, for instance, in cleaner water supplies – and there was a marked reduction in child mortality.

Life expectancy figures represent averages rather than norms, and there were considerable differences in longevity among the grandparents of the Sixty Somethings. Four women recalled grandparents who lived into their eighties or even nineties. 'Even my children knew my grandparents!' said Elizabeth. Two of Liza's grandparents lived into their nineties, even though the grandfather had chain-smoked until he was eighty. According to Tweegy, her octogenarian paternal grandmother had become a kind of object of family veneration: 'She was an invalid and was carried downstairs for our visits. We worshipped her for a bit then went away again.'

Yet such longevity was exceptional. At the other end of the scale were grandparents who had died when the women's parents were children, sometimes leaving families in dire straits. Barbara's maternal grandparents both died of tuberculosis when her mother was very young. Hannah's father lost his mother when he was small. Helen's mother lost hers when she was small. Both Primrose's maternal grandfather's farm-labourer parents were killed, so he was brought up by the Chapel. Norah's paternal grandmother died in 1923 very suddenly: 'heart or something presumably – today they would have picked up on that and it would have been treated and she would have survived into older age.' Stella's maternal grandfather also died young. Katie's father lost his own father to brucellosis at the age of four and his mother to tuberculosis when he was eight. He and his two siblings were raised by a grandmother, an aunt and a cousin. Julia's mother was orphaned altogether at the age of three. Ruby knew her maternal grandmother, who had survived a year and a half in Theresienstadt (a hybrid concentration camp and ghetto near Prague), but all she knew about her father's mother was that 'she was shot into a pit outside Riga' after the Nazi invasion of the former Soviet Union. In later life, Ruby was distressed to read an account of how such killings were carried out.

Not all women had known grandparents, and few had known all four. Even if they had still been alive, they might not have been encountered. Clara's only surviving grandparents, for example, lived in South Africa and were hardly ever seen. Only meeting her real mother at the age of fifty, Lissa seemed never to have known any of her natural grandparents. Furthermore, when her adoptive father left home, her adoptive mother broke off all contact with his parents, a source of some resentment to her. Four women mentioned only ever knowing one grandparent, twelve said they had known two of their grandparents and seven said they had known three.

In other cases, the acquaintance was brief and the memories sketchy and impressionistic, particularly if grandparents died when the Sixty Somethings were still young children. 'She was a very difficult woman,' said Helen of her father's mother. 'I vaguely remember her coming to stay at Christmas, and usually walking out having taken offence.'

Unsurprisingly, the women's engagement with the grandparents they did know varied enormously. In many cases the relationships were particularly supportive, close and loving. Sometimes this involved direct help. When Barbara's mother was teacher-training, her father's Jewish immigrant parents stepped into the breach with childcare. Barbara remembered this as a positive episode. 'They weren't observant, but they did speak Yiddish, so I was introduced to an alternative culture.' And when Bella's mother was suffering from a form of postnatal depression, her own mother, a white Jamaican, came over to England to look after her.

For other families, the closeness was more social. Lilian's mother's unofficially adoptive parents 'lived just a field away, so we saw them every day'. Theresa's father's parents did not live far away. They were 'very much part of the family. I have lots of memories as a real youngster. I was left with them on Saturdays when my parents went to the rugby at Twickenham. We always had Christmas at their house. When you went to stay they had deep feather mattresses so you sank in. Very old-fashioned.' When Theresa's grandfather died, her grandmother came to live with them. Maureen's mother's family had moved to Birmingham from the country. 'We saw quite a lot of them as children. We got put on the coach in Brighton. They were very supportive and cuddly and good and I was very close to my aunt, who lived with them. That was why I went to college in the Midlands.' Melissa remembers her father's parents as 'loving and bubbly. They were poor hard-working people but very much into the extended family. I remember as a child extended family parties. There's never been anything like that since!' Sarah's paternal grandparents were 'great fun. My sister and I both have such happy memories of them. They were very poor, lived in Torquay in a rented house and lived hand-to-mouth, but my grandmother would do anything to keep the family together.' More exotically, Miranda had 'wonderful holidays' every summer with her mother's wealthy parents in Norway, 'a very beautiful country'. Dolly thought her mother's mother was 'feisty' and 'wonderful'. She was 'the person who influenced me most, when I look back. There was always room for someone else at the table, however little food there was. My mother was the same and I'm the same.'

A small minority of grandparents, however, were remembered as distant and unhelpful. Bella's paternal grandmother was 'very much the Victorian'. When Bella's mother arrived in London, newly married, inexperienced and lonely, her mother-in-law was unwelcoming. 'She had lived through two world wars and didn't want to deal with a complete greenhorn.' Stephanie only had one grandparent on each side and they were both very distant. 'We were only to be seen and not heard. I feel very bad when I talk to a lot of people and I hear about lovely, lovely relationships with grandparents and grandchildren and the specialness of that bond. I feel very sad not to have experienced any of that. It was very formal and we had to sit there and be quiet while they chatted away. There was no bond.'

Sometimes it seemed that relationships with grandfathers had been affected by the First World War and the toll it had taken on the family. Deirdre never knew her paternal grandfather because he was killed on his first day in action in France in 1916. Two grandfathers were injured in the Battle of the Somme. One of Audrey's lost an arm, and Katie's was wounded by a shell splinter in his foot, which left him slightly lame for the rest of his life. Theresa's maternal grandfather died from gangrene when an old wound from a shell splinter became infected years later. Bella's grandfather was 'never the same again' after the war. Four of the women believed their grandfathers had returned from the war badly affected by 'shell shock'. The concept dates from this time and the term was first referred to in the *Lancet* in February 1915 to cover a wide range of physical and psychological symptoms. It had been described as 'mental and nervous shock among the wounded' in an earlier editorial to the *British Medical Journal* in November 2014. Definitions change, but we would probably now refer to most such conditions as post-traumatic stress disorder, more often abbreviated to PTSD.

It is impossible to estimate numbers, but the trauma experienced by men sent to the trenches has been well chronicled in historical books and documentaries. A more immediate sense of the experience is to be found in the works of the many war poets of the time, such as Robert Graves, Siegfried Sassoon and Wilfred Owen, who admitted to shell shock himself. The effects of the condition were starkly described in poems like Owen's 'Mental Cases' and Sassoon's 'Survivors'. These and many other poets related the horrors of war and the experience of being at the front.

Grandparents' occupations and standards of living

Many of the Sixty Somethings were able to give some account of their grandparents' occupations. Their reports would seem to reflect the occupational structure of the first half of the twentieth century when, compared to present times, there were greater numbers of semi-skilled and unskilled manual workers and fewer people employed in non-manual work in Britain. As David Glass also charted in his seminal work *Social Mobility in Britain*, published in 1954, more people were also employed in industries such as farming, fishing and mining, with rather fewer in larger industrial organisations than is the case today. The working classes outnumbered the middle classes at that time.

The first half of the twentieth century was also a time of austerity and widespread poverty, albeit with pockets of affluence and wealth. Many families were affected, particularly in the north of the country, by the decline of traditional industries. The severe depression of the 1930s took its toll when up to a quarter of the male workforce was out of work. Public discontent was demonstrated by the General Strike of 1926 as well as the hunger marches of the 1920s and 1930s, notably the Jarrow March of 1936 when shipyard workers marched all the way to London to protest against poverty and unemployment. Conditions began to improve towards the end of the 1930s as food and accommodation became cheaper, work became more plentiful and new industries, such as car and electronics manufacturing, were established. From 1939 all workers became entitled to at least one week's paid holiday entitlement a year, something that they had previously been denied.

Additionally, paid employment at the time was largely a male domain. At the turn of the century the role of the woman was commonly seen as the wife, mother and homemaker, although women were increasingly gaining paid employment. They were also called upon to take part in the war effort, perhaps working in the munitions industry, even if opportunities were more limited for them again once the war came to an end. Unsurprisingly, therefore, only five of the Sixty Somethings recalled grandmothers who worked throughout their adult lives, two because of widowhood, one due to desertion and one after her husband lost his job. It was not explained why the fifth, a Scottish schoolmistress, had carried on working.

Eighteen women described grandparents from distinctly poor working-class homes, including three from mining families. There were mill workers, mechanics, a milkman, a woman who worked in a laundry and another in domestic service. One grandmother with six children worked as a housekeeper to a priest when her husband was sent to prison.

A further eight women said their grandparents had been poor farmers or agricultural labourers. Eleanor said her farmer

AN INHERITANCE: GRANDPARENTS AND PARENTS

grandparents in Cornwall were so hard up they had to 'farm out' her father to another family because they had too many children. Alison's paternal grandmother had married a gamekeeper, who died young, then a railway worker who also died. Twice widowed, she went to live in lodgings in London.

Some women did not specify their grandparents' occupations beyond noting that they were hard-up. Barbara for instance, said her paternal grandparents, first-generation Jewish refugees who only spoke Yiddish, were 'absolutely totally poverty-stricken'.

Certainly, several women were left with striking memories of their grandparents' straitened circumstances, sometimes exacerbated by the number of children. Indeed, the rate of childbearing was high in their generation, at about double the current level. According to information from British Social Trends, families at the turn of the twentieth century had an average completed family size of 3.5 children. This figure, moreover, concealed the very large number of pregnancies of some women. 'My grandparents were really poor!' said Lynne, exemplifying the point. 'Both were from families of ten. When the older ones married, younger ones went to live with them to spread the load.' The daughter of an agricultural worker (a veteran of the Boer War and the First World War), Annie's mother was one of 11 children. Meg's Catholic maternal grandfather was the youngest of 14 children. The surviving elder siblings, of whom she thought there were seven, 'did the Empire thing' and went to Canada, South Africa and the States. He had to stay at home with his aged parents. 'I think he resented it all his life because he was a very bitter, twisted old man.'

Family visits could provide glimpses of a bygone era. Molly's father was one of eight children born to a Scottish farm labourer. 'Their lives would have been totally almost nineteenth-century,' she reflected. 'You'd go and see them in their cottage and there'd be ice on the inside of the windows.' Stella's father came from a farm in Ireland. 'Life was so different. We would go to visit until the 1960s. They had no running water. They got water from a well or a spring, so people carried buckets, which is incredible now. As a child it was exciting, but not so exciting when you're living there 52 weeks a year. They had no electricity until the mid-1960s and they had *nothing*.' However, she noted that her cousins, 'to whom we would take our clothes in the 1960s because they were so poor, have all become very very successful', either in Ireland or abroad. Lilian's illegitimate mother was unofficially adopted by what she described as a 'backstreet midwife' and her millworker husband. 'They were fantastic but they lived in a one-up, one-down cottage with one cold water tap and no loo, just a series of "dry toilets" at the top of the farmyard.'

Such encounters, however brief, left a lingering appreciation of the difficulties faced by the poor in their grandparents' generation. Unemployment was sometimes but by no means always the issue. Life could still be extremely tough for those in steady work. 'My sense of their life is just unbelievably hard work and no choice of anything,' said Meg of her maternal grandparents in the Ayrshire coalfields, where her grandfather managed a gasworks. Her grandmother was 'speechless with pride when my mother bought her a washing machine in the early 1960s that her girl was prosperous enough to afford a washing machine for her mother. It was such a big deal! But also embarrassed because the neighbours would think she was getting above herself. I remember the house she lived in still had the copper in its own little house in the yard, so she'd be hanging all the bedclothes out and doing the washing that way, and this was a woman in her seventies.' In her Northern mining town, Jacca's maternal grandmother 'had to look after hordes of people and get them to school with shoes on their feet. Not enough money and not enough shoes, and the kids had to walk miles to school.'

Most grandparents had less precarious lives, though sometimes only marginally so. Fourteen women had grandparents with skilled working-class or lower-middle-class occupations. These included a chauffeur for the local Co-op, a railwayman, a 'twist-hand' (an important job in a lace factory) and two engineers, one of whom was believed to have been blacklisted in the 1930s 'because he was instrumental in the unions'. There were tradesmen: a painter and decorator and two builders, one of whom travelled abroad building NAAFIs for the British military and another who ran his own small business. Others who ran small businesses included two shopkeepers, one of whom was also a picture-framer, and a publican. One grandfather ran his own haulage company, using horses and carts. There were two sets of farmers (as opposed to farm labourers), though one of these families lost everything during the German occupation of Jersey. Others with regular but modest incomes included a policeman, two Scottish Presbyterian ministers and two schoolteachers.

One of Helen's grandfathers worked his way from 'literally the bottom' of a famous national bank to 'quite high up'.

Yet even among the better-off grandparents the women recall the simplicity and frugality of their lives. Hannah and her parents lived in her father's 90-year-old grandmother's house, along with Hannah's grandfather, the haulage contractor. Her great-grandmother had gone there as a bride and lived in one room as a bedsit. 'She had gas mantles and a fire where you put the kettle on the fire – she used to talk to the telephone.' Tabitha actually enjoyed the simplicity of her maternal grandparents' lives. They were 'the model of stability' with a typical routine: 'Monday you did the washing; Tuesday you did the ironing; Wednesday you did the baking …' and so on. 'A woman was totally occupied all day, keeping the house together.' This routine 'was great for a child with restless parents!' When Persia visited her mother's parents, they had to make their own entertainment because there was no TV. 'It used to be lovely going up there as children because there were all kinds of things for us to do, very inventive things involving teamwork.'

Eighteen women's grandfathers had more clearly middle-class or professional occupations. These included a pharmacist, a university academic who became a college principal, a doctor, a bank manager, a captain in the Royal Artillery who went on to work in a bank and the bishop of a prestigious Anglican diocese.

Those in business included a travelling salesman, first for British Petroleum, then for Vickers Aircraft, a wool merchant, a woollen mill owner, the owner/manager of a large building firm and a grandfather who owned a business in Birmingham and became the mayor of Droitwich. They were not all equally successful. Sylvie's maternal grandfather was a businessman 'but,' she said, 'he was absolutely hopeless at it.' One woman's paternal grandparents were descended from a Victorian politician. Her mother, though, was from country gentry.

Some were harder to pigeonhole. Primrose's paternal grandfather was a wealthy American industrialist. Her grandmother was an heiress who would have been wealthy until, Primrose said, her husband lost all her money. Tweegy described her paternal grandfather as 'a man of independent means' who never worked but never seemed to have any money.

Social mobility in the grandparental generation

Few women talked about the social origins of their grandparents as these were usually too distant for them to have much knowledge. Three, however, suggested they had experienced little social mobility. Skelton, for instance, told how her father's parents lived in the house her grandmother had been born in until they died. Both she and Chenhalls implied a long family work history spanning several generations, in coal mining and the steelworks for the former, and farming for the latter. Others apparently had aspirations to be middle class, even if they didn't achieve it. Poppy's grandfather, for instance, had set up a private care hire business and owned three cars. Her husband had pointed out to her that he had in fact been a taxi driver, something she said she hadn't quite twigged before. Sylvie also mentioned her grandfather, whom she'd always been told was a bookkeeper. He had in fact been a bookmaker.

There were a few women, nonetheless, who could point to significant gains in social status among their grandparents themselves. These included a grandmother from a poor Scottish farming background who rose to become a matron in a big hospital and a grandfather from a working-class family in Manchester who became 'a very successful businessman. Very rich by the time he finished.' Among the most dramatic risers was Primrose's maternal grandfather. 'His parents were farm labourers in Wales, so very low in the social pecking order. They were both killed, so he was brought up by the Chapel and apprenticed to be a butcher. He went to night school and eventually became one of the most renowned solicitors in North Wales.' One of his sons became an MP, 'the Minister for Wales and Leader of the House of Commons.' Another was 'President of the Oxford Old Boys' Society'.

Some grandparents were of course overtly aspirational. Jo's maternal grandmother was a case in point. She pushed her children to join the tennis club and go to elocution classes. A former seamstress, she made them 'beautiful clothes from scraps of rubbish in order to better their lives'. In complete contrast, Zena's paternal grandfather, 'according to various sources', had been an aspiring politician with the IRA. 'We tried to find him mentioned in despatches, but his name is sadly missing. Family myths are wonderful!'

Sex, marriage and parenthood in the early twentieth century

The early twentieth century was an era when extramarital sex, infidelity and illegitimacy were generally frowned upon even if, as Pat Thane and Tanya Evans detailed in their 2013 study entitled *Sinners? Scroungers? Saints?: Unmarried Motherhood in Twentieth-Century England*, cohabitation and children born of unmarried parents were acknowledged by law in terms of legal protection for children and workers. Official statistics on these arrangements and other aspects of sexual behaviour were not recorded until very many years later, except to some degree in Scotland. Nonetheless, cohabitation was widely reported by historians, such as by Charles Booth in his 1889 *Life and Labour of the People in London* and subsequent works. In general, much more was known about working-class than middle-class lives at this time.

Undoubtedly being born out of wedlock could bring hardship for the grandparents of the Sixty Somethings. Frances's maternal grandmother was illegitimate. 'She had a very hard upbringing, which my mother talked about a lot.' Such situations could even lead to complete ostracism. Jenny's maternal grandmother 'was married and had three kids, then her husband died of pneumonia when she was forty and they were living with his parents. I understand she had an affair and got pregnant and they were all kicked out.' As a consequence, Jenny's mother had to leave grammar school 'which she always resented. My grandmother never had anywhere to live.' Eventually she got dementia and went into 'a horrendous mental hospital'. Jenny met her illegitimate half-sister for the first time at her second cousin's funeral.

Hayley's maternal grandfather's story was also extreme. 'He had been found in a laundry basket on the doorstep of a parish priest with half a playbill saying "Please take care of my baby", which made him convinced he was the son of a famous actor.' He was immediately adopted by an Irish family in Croydon. Hayley thought he was almost certainly the son of one of the daughters in the family. He had a career as a Civil Servant, but Hayley believed his illegitimacy still held him back because 'you couldn't get beyond a certain point if you didn't have a birth certificate.' Maggie's maternal grandmother was deserted by her soldier husband 'at a time when it was really not on to be a single parent and working. My mother and her sister used to pretend at school that everything was normal at home.'

Eleanor's mother was illegitimate because her parents had a different problem. Her grandfather had married a Roman

Catholic woman who ran off with another man, but because she was Catholic she couldn't divorce him. Eleanor's grandparents then met, her grandmother fell pregnant with her mother and they set up house together (Eleanor wasn't sure which came first). 'When Mother was three she was farmed out to relatives. Mum says they couldn't possibly have kept me because of the scandal. She remembered coming back from school and asking her auntie what "bastard" meant, from the playground.' She didn't live with her parents again until she was twelve or thirteen.

Such attitudes, which may seem harsh today, were widespread at the time and crossed class boundaries. Zena's maternal grandmother 'seemingly came from an affluent family. She ran off with my grandfather, who was a sailor and had six children. He died when the youngest, my mum, was six months old. She was left destitute and her family still wouldn't acknowledge her. She had contravened the family code.'

From a wealthy family, Primrose's paternal grandmother, still only seventeen, became an army driver in the First World War. She was assigned to Primrose's grandfather, a wealthy industrialist. They fell in love and he seduced her. She got pregnant in 1921 and she went over to America because she didn't want my father to appear on English birth records. 'My grandfather had a family in America. I think he was a bit of a lad. So my grandmother had my father in America. I really loved her. She was an extraordinary woman. She said that she and her own mother (Primrose's great-grandmother) had gone over by boat. They had to disguise the fact that my grandmother was pregnant and they sang on the way a song current at the time "And Her Mother Came Too", so they obviously got into the fun part of it as well.' Eventually Primrose's American grandfather came to live with her grandmother in England, but they would not acknowledge Primrose's father while they were still unmarried. He was brought up by two female nurses in Brighton until he was seven, when the grandparents were finally able to marry and brought him to their home.

The legacy left by grandparents

Most grandparents left some kind of emotional legacy. Those who were loved or respected became positive role models for the Sixty Somethings, while others were objects of dislike whose examples were to be avoided.

Often it was the sheer strength of personality that was admired. 'My grandmother was a very strong and important person in my mother's life,' said Jo. Audrey's maternal grandmother was 'an extremely strong-willed independent person. Her grandfather was absolutely unable to engage with his children and could not cope with having them around.' Her grandmother 'did everything and held it all together'. Others had responded to adversity with pragmatic resourcefulness. When Norah's shell-shocked maternal grandfather had to sign on in the Depression, her grandmother, 'a very powerful woman', supported the family by running a boarding house, taking in paying guests. 'Actually, she had a private hotel.' Her grandfather did the accounts, 'but she was the boss'.

Alison's maternal grandmother was another case in point. She and her husband had owned their own small terraced house, and when he had died she had let out rooms to prison warders. Their presence 'made her feel safe'. After she became widowed for a second time, Alison's maternal grandmother went to work in a cartographer and printer's office, delighting her grandchildren by bringing home free Christmas annuals.

Maggie's grandmother was another example. When deserted by her husband she taught herself genealogy and worked at Somerset House for years. Never remarrying, she was 'a very independent working woman', 'quite a role model' and unlike other people's grandmothers who were 'sitting at home knitting'.

Some grandparents seemed quite formidable. Beth's paternal grandmother 'was known as a curmudgeonly old bag' who founded the Shropshire branch of the Women's Institute, campaigned to get electricity in the village and had a suffragist badge. Meg's maternal grandfather may have been 'bitter and twisted', but 'he was also a very principled person.' He managed a gasworks which supplied much of the Ayrshire coalfields and kept it open during the General Strike 'because it was winter and he would not let people's homes freeze.' Meg's mother and brother got beaten up by miners' children because he was perceived as a blackleg.

Overly censorious, puritanical or joyless grandparents were particularly resented. Patricia's paternal grandfather in Northern Ireland 'was a very strict Presbyterian who my father didn't like very much'. Her grandmother, on the other hand, was 'a very sweet, lovely woman'. Jan's father's Scottish Presbyterian parents were 'quite strict and severe'. They were also teetotal. 'My grandfather left the table once when a bottle of wine was put on it. Mother said they'd had a teetotal wedding, which she found very difficult. It was one of the reasons they moved away from Scotland. Mother thought, "I'm not going to stay up here. We need to move south."'

Flavia's maternal grandmother was 'unbelievably tight-lipped and very Victorian in her outlook'. Her grandfather, who died when Flavia was about two, was 'an absolutely gorgeous man who had a wonderful sense of humour and wrote her notes in rhyme. But she would have none of it.' She was a rigid disciplinarian with Flavia's mother, who was the second of five children 'and found it very difficult'. In possible mitigation, Flavia said that she had only just learned that her grandfather 'drank a lot and was a bit of a roué'.

Similarly, Winifred's maternal grandmother 'was very fierce and strict, really not a pleasant person to visit. She didn't like children really, so she would try to get us out of the house as soon as possible – there was a little park nearby – so my mother was just left visiting her on her own. Everything we did was found fault with. I don't know quite what we were expected to do. We weren't naughty children – I know my younger sister felt even more strongly about this than I did. She absolutely hated my grandmother. And she was a very bad mother to my mum as well. She pretty much abandoned my mother, who was an only child.' Nevertheless, Winifred's mum ended up as her demented mother's main carer.

Even puritanical grandparents could be much loved. Katie told how her father had recalled his first Christmas with his in-laws. His wife's parents never drank except for making a single jug of shandy to drink with Christmas dinner. When Katie's mother poured herself a second glass, her father was shocked, saying, 'Don't go haphazard with that liquor!' Strict morality also meant he refused to lend the young man his library ticket because it said 'Not Transferable'. These stories were told with amused affection.

Other grandparents were remembered for their lifestyle or personality. Liza's grandparents 'didn't believe in exercise. They lived off their garden basically. Everything was exactly the same: sausages on Monday, ham on Tuesday, etc. She boiled her vegetables for an hour.' Frances's maternal grandfather was a miner who lived with them briefly when she was in her teens. 'He didn't read and didn't talk much about anything except sport: Notts

County and the horses. He didn't have a good relationship with my mother and I was taught to disregard what he said, though he was very popular with other people.'

Both Geraldine's grandmothers were unusual. Her father's Italian mother was 'a smoking Catholic with high heels. Very glamorous. She tried to talk to us about Catholicism and paint our nails. Mother was not pleased!' A contrast was her mother's mother, who 'lived with the family for a bit, a Christian Scientist. An unusual woman.'

Some unknown grandparents were attractive for their reputations. Frances never knew her maternal grandfather's illegitimate first wife, who was 'a woman I'd probably have clicked with, who read widely and was a suffragist'. Unlike her father's dour parents, Jan's mother came from 'a much more artistic family. I have this fantasy that I'd have got on well with them, a family that liked enjoying life.' Molly thought her mother's mother 'was clearly pretty wild. She obviously had a lot of personality. Very strong. They used to do a lot of arguing, but they still loved each other. I think the genetic connection went from her to my aunt and has come down to me. She used to do amazing, wild crochet and knitting in the sixties and seventies so she was "with it".'

According to Hayley, her grandfather was 'the black sheep of the family'. He was a good singer, who went round pubs entertaining. 'I like to think I'm like my grandfather even though he was a naughty man. He was very feckless and her grandmother had a terrible time. He would go to the pub on Friday night and forget to come home for three days. When he came back it wasn't with something useful like food, but perhaps a pair of French knickers or something ridiculously useless.'

Sylvie's maternal grandfather may have been 'hopeless' at business, but he was an eccentric and 'a most wonderful man.

His whole life was Shakespeare. He wasn't educated. He hadn't been to university. He was a prison visitor and he believed that if they understood Shakespeare that would be the making of them. And he'd go down to Oxford – if he'd read a book by Bradley or Tawney or someone, he'd go and knock on their door. He knew Walter de la Mare and Augustus John, a sort of little Bloomsbury in the North. He loved walking. He just walked and walked and walked and took me with him. He was absolutely delightful. I was very lucky.'

Unsurprisingly, many women found their grandparents' world views old-fashioned and conservative, many conditioned by religion, though there were often contrasts between different sets of grandparents. Jemima's father's parents were 'very conventional in their views', but her mother's mother became a suffragette (one of three grandmothers reported to support the movement). Her maternal grandparents had lived in China and Russia. They were 'very travelled, interesting people' with a 'much more global view'. Similarly, Melissa's grandmother was 'very interested in the world and in politics and would listen to the news'.

Audrey's maternal grandmother had very strong views, 'not necessarily views I adhere to. She was a feminist in her way, but also conservative, strongly involved in the church but felt female clergy were an anathema.' Olive's father's parents had very strong attitudes towards drink. Neither drank and they supported traditional religion, though 'I don't know how much it meant to them'. According to Meg, religion was very important in the Ayrshire coalfields. There was 'a huge sense of community among people who never travelled further than fifty miles from where they lived, along with deference to royalty and the government'. Mary's mother's parents were 'scandalised by all sorts of things that even my mother would say. Very Victorian in their approach to life.' Lynne thought her mother's parents had no education and were 'very narrow-minded'. Liza's grandparents 'adored the Royal Family'.

Although there were mixed feelings, many Sixty Somethings expressed appreciation of their grandparents. In Meg's words, 'My grandparents were amazing people. I feel such gratitude. I wish I'd known them better at an age when I could have said to them, "Thanks for everything."'

Education: an opportunity for parents

Another legacy of the grandparents was, of course, their children, the parents of the Sixty Somethings. Some of these women, however, knew little or nothing about their parents' early lives. Eleanor, for instance, knew her father had been 'farmed out' to another family by his impoverished parents in rural Cornwall, but said she 'never heard anyone talking about my father's teenage years. I don't know if they even existed!' He went on to run his own shop, becoming a telephone operator when that didn't work out.

What many of the Sixty Somethings did report on, however, was the significance of education in their parents' generation. Schooling to the age of 14 had been free and compulsory for all since the 'Fisher' Education Act of 1918, but before the 'Butler' Act of 1944 opportunities for secondary or further education were extremely limited, especially for the poor. Getting precious places in grammar schools could transform lives. From 'a poor background in Devon', Sarah's father went to grammar school, which was 'a big heave up'. He joined Marks and Spencer, eventually becoming a store manager at different locations around the country.

Others too benefited enormously from education, with those fathers making the most striking upward social journeys seeming to fall into four main categories. There were 'scholarship boys' who found their way into grammar schools and thence, perhaps, to university, in several cases with the help of benevolent outside intervention. There were self-improvers who took advantage of later educational opportunities like night-school classes. There were career-builders who worked their way up within organisations. And there were self-made entrepreneurs who built up their own businesses.

When Alison's paternal grandmother was widowed twice, she earned money as a cleaner in 'various big houses'. One belonged to a doctor 'who was very kind towards my father and helped him out a bit because he saw my father was a bright boy and had potential'. Even so, her father was only able to go to the grammar school, Alison said, 'because one of his teachers lent him the money for the uniform. Otherwise he wouldn't have been able to go.' After matriculation, someone in the grammar school 'pushed him in the direction of the civil service, and that's what he did, straight after school'.

In his privately published autobiography *Catching the Rope: A Memoir of the Early Years 1918–1946*, the late Sir Roy Shaw, who was brought up in extreme poverty in Sheffield and rose to become the Secretary General of the Arts Council, likened such acts of kindly mentoring to throwing a rope to a boy struggling in the water. Jo's father was another such rope-catcher. With his own father in prison, his Irish mother was working as housekeeper to a Catholic priest. 'Dad was a little intellectual prodigy,' she said. 'The priest took an interest in him and pushed him towards a Catholic school. He got a scholarship there and then a scholarship to Cambridge.'

When Katie's father failed the exams for grammar school, his elementary school headmaster went to the city's education office with examples of his work and insisted they reconsider. As a result he was awarded a scholarship to grammar school and never looked back. Not everyone was fortunate enough to be thrown a rope, though. Annie said her father won a scholarship to art college but could not afford to go.

For Jan's strict Presbyterian family in Scotland, 'academic success was strong in the household. It was what everyone aspired to.' Her father 'would have gone to an Academy School', she said, 'the Scottish equivalent of a grammar school'. He became a GP. Minnie describes her father's parents as 'lower middle class or upper working class, but quite aspirational and very keen for their one son to get a good education. They saved and moved to an area where he could go to a prep school, so he could get into a grammar school.' They were delighted, she reported, when he became an officer in the Royal Navy.

According to Molly her father's family of agricultural labourers were 'proper working class', but he attended Madras College, then a type of grammar school in St Andrews. When he joined the army as a junior officer, 'they thought he'd been in India because he'd been to Madras College and assigned him to the Indian army.' After the war, he made his career in the army, eventually becoming a major in the military police.

Melissa's father was one of the self-improvers. The son of a skilled worker in engineering, he 'went up the ladder', she said. 'He did further education while working and then progressed to a management role – so would be considered middle class.' He became a constructional engineer, 'always trying to go another step up the ladder'. Persia's father was another example. She did not describe his background, but told how he left school at fourteen, went to night school and 'had to bring himself up'. Eventually he became a director in a large construction company. Both Barbara's parents might fall into this category, taking advantage of a post-war training scheme to enter the teaching profession.

Those who worked their way up within organisations included Lilian's father, who left school at 12 and spent his whole working life in the Yorkshire woollen industry, starting as a clerk and eventually becoming a qualified accountant. Similarly, Robin's father had wished to continue his education but his parents wanted him to leave and get a job. So he left school at sixteen, only to be called up. Eventually he became a technical sales manager for a manufacturer of specialist instrumentation, some used in the oil industry. He did an Open University degree much later in life. The son of impoverished Jewish refugees, Rachel's father was a self-made tradesman who built up his own wood-turning business. Jane's parents joined forces to run a number of business ventures that included catering and antiques.

Others were not so fortunate. The son of a chauffeur for the

Co-op, Lynne's father was expected to go out to work and follow her grandfather into the company. 'There was no money to go to school.' Eventually, however, he became a 'Way-Leave Officer', negotiating rights of way for power lines for the Electricity Board. Persia's mother's education was limited as she had to leave her grammar school early when it closed in the afternoons for military use. 'She was always considered the bright one,' but her generation 'never had the opportunities we had. They really had to educate themselves, whereas I was educated.' Although raised as a Christian in Germany, Ruby's mother's education was abruptly curtailed when her Jewish heritage meant she was no longer allowed to attend school after the Nazis came to power. 'Mother didn't know she was Jewish until she had to do all these things like wear a star and an armband and not go to school. I think she lived in shock for the rest of her life. She had no Jewish teaching at all.'

Education did not appear to be of similar importance to all the Sixty Somethings' mothers. Sarah said hers 'was at some awful boarding school, where she heard them say "Your brains are in your feet."' She became a ballet dancer. Jo's mother 'was born working class and very beautiful. Her very ambitious mother sent her to elocution lessons, grooming her to marry a banker or a dentist. But she married someone from her own class.' Julia did not discuss her mother's education but told how 'she was orphaned at three and brought up by a maiden aunt who spent the money on medicines and things'. Somewhere along the road she acquired the skills to become a dance, mime and voice-production tutor. Hazel Grace's mother may have been from a wealthier country background, but 'she was not highly educated', just 'very bright and spectacularly pretty'.

The Second World War

The concept of the 'baby boom' implicitly acknowledges the fact that the Second World War was a massive interruption to normal life, a national crisis straddling a crucial six years of one generation's young adult lives. For the Sixty Somethings' parents, education and nascent careers alike could be delayed or sometimes completely curtailed. New relationships might be formed; existing relationships could be damaged or even destroyed. Inevitably the process of starting families was often postponed until the peace, when this demographic bottle was finally uncorked.

Many Sixty Somethings were acutely aware of the significance of the war in their parents' lives. It was almost always a time of disruption, a time of tragedy for some and of exhilaration and self-discovery for others. 'Their childhood stopped at seventeen,' Jemima said of her parents. 'They were very grown-up at twenty-one, because of fighting in a war.' 'The war was a chunk of their youth – absolutely crucial,' added Betty. Her parents 'went through the war and that shaped their lives'. According to Helen, 'the war was a huge factor in my own parents' lives – *huge*. They got married in 1941 but were apart for four years, so my mother was not very young when she had children.'

Knowledge of this crucial difference in experience between themselves and their parents coloured many Sixty Somethings' views of their own lives, leaving a residue of appreciation and even something akin to 'survivor guilt'. 'The war was an experience for our parents which we did not have to examine,' reflected Margaret. 'They had to live through the war, which had the most colossal effect on everything they did until the day they died,' added Jo of her parents. 'That is completely underestimated.

They didn't want to talk about the war because it was all so awful, so we had to find it out gradually. I feel guilty that I spent my first thirty years being ignorant of the sacrifices their generation made.' 'We've emerged because of the way the war changed things for our parents,' Molly commented. 'Because we hadn't been in the war, I don't think we appreciated what our parents were giving us.' 'Their lives were shaped by the war,' said Sarah. They made 'huge sacrifices'. Elizabeth felt her parents always 'lived in the shadow of the war'.

There was much awareness of the hardships many parents had endured in this period. 'The fact that there was a war going on when my parents met and married meant they had a very difficult start to their life together,' observed Robin. 'The war threw a lot of stuff up in the air and changed it a lot,' reflected Mary, 'rationing and all that sort of thing. I picked up a lot of that feeling. I can't bear wasting anything.' 'My parents' lives were austere and difficult during the war,' said Maureen. 'Money was short. There was rationing. We were so lucky during our lives compared to them.'

Not everyone was equally affected, however. As farmers, Chenhalls' family were 'better off than most' during both world wars. 'They were less affected by rationing and there was a market for anything they could produce.'

For Meg the collective effort was a source of admiration: 'They knew exactly what they were fighting for. It was a huge thing: the country pulling together.' According to Norah her parents' lives 'seemed to be defined by the six years of the war. It was really the most significant part of their lives. When my father died my mother wanted his rank and the fact that he was in the airborne division put on his gravestone. He was demobbed in 1946 and after that he'd done loads, but that was how she thought of him really.'

National Service was in operation between 1939 and 1960, referred to as War Service until 1948, and by 1942 all men aged between 18 and 51 were liable to be called up. There were exemptions for the medically unfit, those in certain specified occupations and anyone accepted as a conscientious objector, but for the majority of adult males there was the unavoidable reality that they might be required to fight. For women the situation was rather different. A second National Service Act of 1941 widened conscription to all unmarried and widowed women without children between the ages of 20 and 30. Although these women could be called up, none of the Sixty Somethings mentioned that this had been the case in their families.

The fathers' experience of war varied enormously. Molly's father joined the army from Madras College 'to avoid being a "Bevan Boy" and going down the mines'. Audrey's father was an army padre. He kept a diary until his death at 70, and it is clear from the wartime entries that 'this was when he was truly alive'. Eleanor described her father as 'a radio expert'.

Theresa's father was in the Royal Engineers 'at the tail end of the war'. 'My father's life was interrupted by war,' said Tabitha. 'He was nearly three years in the Middle East in the ground division of the RAF. I think they had it very tough.' Katie's father was in the anti-aircraft artillery, based first in North Africa and later in Naples. Norah's father 'in the airborne' landed on D-Day then won the MC and was wounded on the Rhine crossing. 'It certainly affected him because he lost dear friends.'

Norah's mother's father was one of several grandfathers who were still active in World War Two. He had been in the army in the First World War and was in the Air Force in the Second. 'He always said if there was a Third World War, he'd join the Navy. I think for him being in uniform was a happy experience!' After Patricia's grandfather died, 'we found a picture of him at the liberation of Belsen,' she said. 'I think he was sent in as an independent observer.' Mary's wealthy businessman grandfather was 'involved in all sorts of secret stuff ... He used to travel extensively on the continent before the war broke out and invented the proximity fuse (used to explode missiles close to their targets).'

Several parents endured personal tragedies. Both Sylvie's mother's life and her grandparents' lives 'were blighted by war', she said. 'It was incredibly significant. Their aspirations were hampered by what they had to do, and they experienced great sorrow because they lost people.' 'Both my mother and father lost family members in the war,' added Jemima, whose maternal grandparents 'lost everything' in the Nazi occupation of Jersey. Julia's mother had been engaged to someone who was killed in the war, while Sarah's mother's first husband was a Lancaster pilot, shot down and killed while she was pregnant with Sarah's older sister. 'She was a widowed mother, living in London during the Blitz with a small baby. Life was very difficult.' Then she met someone on VE night and remarried.

Brought up by adoptive parents, Lissa's story was particularly poignant. Her natural mother was married to a pilot who was killed in the war. She later met an American in the US Army Air Force. After the war he went back to America, where he had a wife and young child. She did not tell him that she was pregnant with Lissa. 'She was being supported by her late husband's parents and feared if they knew she'd had a baby out of wedlock they wouldn't support her any more, so she gave Lissa up for adoption.' Lissa did not rediscover her natural mother until she herself was in her fifties, when they seemed to form a strong bond. Tabitha's mother found the war exciting in a rather different way: 'It was the best time of her life,' Tabitha said. 'She left home at 17 to go into the WRAF (Women's Royal Air Force). They were all young recruits. Mother met and married an American GI, but never made it to the boat to go to America. She divorced him and married my father. My mother's character was all about a hedonistic lifestyle. The war was very good for these sorts of people because I imagine there was a feeling that "you'd better do it today". And whereas earlier or later society might have frowned on this pleasure-seeking, then I imagine it was regarded as only sensible.'

Perhaps the most spectacular wartime romance belonged to Miranda's parents. Her father parachuted into his future wife's garden in Norway, according to legend, getting tangled up in a washing line. 'My mother's grandfather was a famous man in Oslo,' Miranda said. 'He held a banquet at the end of the war where he invited all the English soldiers. My father was seen as a great hero. My mother was twelve years younger. They fell in love and got married very quickly in this huge celebration. A lot of Norwegian–English marriages happened at that time.' Somewhat less dramatically, perhaps, Jan's parents met in Hamburg after the war, where 'my father was helping with the recovery'.

Mothers: education and work before children

For some young women who became the mothers of the Sixty Somethings, the war provided an unwelcome interruption to their education. 'Had the war not come along I think Mother was going to study economics,' reported Maggie, 'but none of that ever happened.' Persia's mother left her grammar school after getting ten O levels, dismayed that the school day had been reduced to mornings only because the building was taken over by the military in the afternoons. 'She joined the Ministry of Labour and called people up.' Meg's mother had 'what would be described as "a good war" in that she had an interesting army career. But in many ways her choices were reduced to practically nothing, first by economics and then by the war.'

The First World War had seen millions of women taking jobs previously performed by men, especially in the munitions industry, and something similar happened during the Second World War. For many of the mothers of the Sixty Somethings it provided early experience of paid work, and for some this proved a time of self-discovery. Katherine's mother had already done a year's nurse training, but when war started she worked in armaments factories and then the woollen mills in Yorkshire. Lindyloo's mother was in the Land Army (young women recruited as agricultural workers) and both she and Deirdre's mother drove ambulances. Helen's mother was a 'VAD', a nurse with the Volunteer Aid Detachment, 'her only ever job', and Betty's mother was a fire warden. Norah's mother was in the Air Force: 'It seemed to have defined her life.'

For a few, war-work provided a time of new excitement. Audrey thought her mother 'loved the war. She had a very good time.' Jemima's 'very very clever' mathematician mother may have had her education curtailed, but she was recruited to work for MI5 at Blenheim Palace. Alison's mother worked in various offices during the war, ending up operating teleprinters in a building called The Citadel (the massive concrete military communications bunker still next to the Admiralty Arch on The Mall). 'She said they used to have all sorts of larks during their breaks, sending messages to people they shouldn't have and linking up with the States somehow.'

Theresa felt her mother, the youngest of a family of seven, had not been very happy at home. 'She escaped to join the Wrens [Women's Royal Naval Service] when she was about eighteen in 1944. She loved that and never went back home. She was sent to Bletchley Park. Nobody knew she was there. She never told anyone for fifty years. One Sunday morning over breakfast there was something in the papers about it as fifty years had passed. She said to Dad, "I was there!" He'd never known. She thought she'd be shot if she told anyone. She operated the "Bombs" [Alan Turing's then state-of-the-art codebreaking computers]. Three shifts a day. She didn't meet anyone in the other shifts. Her parents never asked where she was. She accepted that she wasn't to know. I wonder if that would work now!' Later Theresa took her mother to visit Bletchley Park. 'She was taken into a back room and invited to start up a working Bomb. And she did. She could still do it.'

Although the First World War is believed to have boosted the movement to grant the vote to women as the war went through its final stages in 1918, there was no comparable ensuing sociopolitical shift after the Second World War. If anything, the post-war period saw mounting pressure on women to return to the home. Despite the great range of women's war work, this was still an era when they were generally expected to give up paid employment when they married, or at least when the first child arrived. Whatever they had done in the past, their social status was now likely to be determined by their husband's occupation. Alice's grandmother, for example, was born into a poor rural family and rose to lower-middle-class respectability as a hospital matron. As the wife of a GP, Alice's mother became a somewhat uncomfortable recruit to the professional middle classes.

Despite the widespread assumption that women should aim to become full-time wives and mothers, twenty-five Sixty

Somethings said their mothers had had some kind of paid employment in their early adult life. Lindyloo's mother, for example, had been 'in service somewhere in Eastbourne before her war work', and Alison's mother did not work after her wartime job in the Citadel. Katherine's mother however continued as a mill-worker.

Certain jobs had long been considered more appropriate for young women. Theresa's mother, for instance, 'was a hairdresser for a short time'. Ruby's mother had trained as a nurse, and Carol and Lilian's mothers had both worked in shops. Carol's mother had also done clerical work, as had Persia's mother for the Ministry of Defence. Tweegy said her mother had worked in an office, Robin's had been a secretary, and Melissa's had had a more specialist office role as a 'comptometer operator', trained to use an early form of business calculator. Violet's mother had been a civil servant.

Others followed professions. Winifred's mother worked as an architect before the war. Later, 'she had my sister and stopped working.' The mothers of Betty, Charlotte, Frances, Jan, Jude and Katie had all been teachers, although Betty's mother was also a radiographer. Geraldine's mother was a graduate in dairy technology, who worked for the Milk Marketing Board before going to Tanzania with her agronomist husband. Four mothers had begun artistic careers before starting their families. Jo's mother and Eleanor's mother had been actresses, Sarah's a ballet dancer until her first pregnancy, while Julia's mother had been a dance, mime and voice-production tutor. Julia felt that had been 'quite an exciting, fulfilling life'. Verity's mother and father ran a business. 'She was the company secretary. She was Italian so she was bilingual. She did languages at a polytechnic and went to work at Thomas Cook. When the war came she went to work in the family restaurant, then married my father and went into business with him.'

Fourteen women said their mothers had never done any paid work at all, even before marriage. Minnie's mother, for example, never had a job. 'She did nursing training but didn't take to it. She left school with next to no qualifications, left home as soon as she could, married and had a family.' Apart from prevailing societal norms, the question of where the pressure for the women to give up work came from was not always clear-cut. After the war Katie's mother taught part-time in a teacher-training college, but stopped when she had her first child. Two decades later Katie's father was indignant when a zealous late-1960s feminist accused him of having a patriarchal marriage because his wife had not had a career of her own. He would have been perfectly happy for her to continue working, he said. The decision to stop work had been entirely her own. Katie's mother later admitted that this was not entirely true. She had stopped work fearing the fierce disapproval, not of her husband, but of her own father. Some women, of course, continued to work whilst bringing up their families, often becoming assistants to their husbands. The Sixty Somethings talk about these jobs in the next chapter.

Social mobility between grandparents and parents

Many Sixty Somethings said there was more difference in social status between their grandparents and parents than there was between their parents and themselves. Indeed, and while all the women can loosely be described as middle class, twenty-four spoke of grandparents living in poor circumstances, some in abject poverty, but only one reported a father with an unskilled working-class job, and even that was temporary. Although a number of the Sixty Somethings grew up in impoverished circumstances, no parents seemed to experience the extreme poverty of their own parents as adults. Seven fathers with skilled working-class jobs represented the more modest end of the spectrum of parents' occupations and included a gardener, a fireman, a factory engineer, a storeman and a crane driver.

Sixteen of the women explicitly said their parents had been upwardly mobile socially. Winifred's father, for example, was born into a working-class family but went on to run his own architecture practice. Raised in respectable poverty by his widowed grandmother, Katie's orphaned father became a university lecturer, later holding a senior post in an international agency before becoming the principal of a college of London University.

Fifteen women described grandfathers in skilled working-class or lower-middle-class occupations, the same number as said their fathers were in jobs of this status. But this does not mean these families were socially static. Some had moved from relative poverty to the lower middle classes. Others had moved from the lower to the professional middle classes. Helen's grandfather had worked his way up from the bottom in a national bank. Her father became a WS (Writer to Her Majesty's Signet), a solicitor in Scotland.

Early steps up the social ladder could be comparable for men and women, especially when grandparents were eager for their daughters to be educated. Meg's mother did what she calls 'the Kinnock thing', becoming the first in her family to go to university. 'My grandmother insisted on my mother going to university,' said Meg. 'She saved up her own money from housekeeping because my grandfather refused to give her the money, saying, "The boys need to go to university for professions and you don't." So there was a feminist thing going on there.

Mother went to Glasgow University and became an athlete and a Scottish champion.'

Frances's and Katie's mothers were also the first in their families to go to university. Frances's mother was awarded a miner's scholarship to Kings College London. Katie's mother was the only child of an elementary schoolmaster in a Northern mill town. Her parents had somehow found the money to send her to a prestigious girls' grammar school, then on to university. Generally though, education for women could be altogether more patchy, whatever their background. Jemima's mother was 'very very clever, a mathematician and a gifted pianist, but there was no money for her to go to university.' Raised in great poverty, Lynne's mother 'went to the National School and left at fourteen. She only learned her "Three Rs" working at lace factories and the Co-op.' Barbara described her impoverished mother as largely 'self-educated'.

Those parents born into middle- or upper-middle-class families generally seem to have maintained their social status, even if, like Primrose's father, they went through a period of financial hardship. Chenhalls's parents continued the family tradition of farming. Sylvie's mother was the daughter of the 'absolutely hopeless businessman', but from a family that was 'middle class through and through'. All Sylvie knew about her education was that she 'got to university somehow'. The son of an Anglican bishop, Miranda's father was sent to an elite private school and went on to be headmaster of a famous direct-grant grammar school. Hazel Grace's father attended an equally renowned boarding school, then, after a career as a writer, held a senior position at the BBC.

Mary's mother's family were well off, but she suspected her paternal grandparents 'may have been more like us. I think

Father's mother was a trained pharmacist from Wales and although there was a string of miners on that side, there was also a string of teachers and pharmacists.' Her paternal grandfather was a pharmacist as well, and her own father became a surgeon.

Life after the war

The war left a lasting legacy in the form of altered beliefs and attitudes for many parents of the Sixty Somethings. Audrey's father ceased to be a clergyman and became a civil servant. Lindyloo's father became an atheist. Some may have been keen to restore what they saw as pre-war normality. Others were determined to change society for the better. Barbara's parents both joined a post-war 'crash teacher-training programme', her father a committed communist. Jo said her parents were deeply affected by 'the social revolutions that occurred before and after the war'. Her father made a career in the RAF, where his working-class background and left-wing views did not sit well with most of his colleagues. Katie's Labour-supporting father was berated as a 'Commie' after an argument with a group of travelling salesmen in a cheap guest house in his first job after the war.

The end of the war also signalled a return to a more normal life. The Sixty Somethings' fathers donned their 'demob suits' and returned to a country of severe rationing, 'utility' furniture, 'waste not, want not' and 'make do and mend'. Clement Attlee's new Labour government was trying to plan a National Health Service while struggling with the problems of withdrawal from empire, economic rebuilding and the sheer enormity of the national debt. There were fuel shortages too, just when the country was hit by an unprecedentedly bitter winter. At least the young men were ready to start, or resume, their careers.

Many young women were, however, giving up work, whether willingly or not, and turning their attentions to their homes and families. The question of whether it was better for a woman to have an independent career or not was to become a central point of comparison between the Sixty Somethings and their mothers. Many would grow up to question whether their mothers had made the best choice at this crucial juncture in their lives.

Then the baby boom began.

3

Growing Up

All the Sixty Somethings were born during the two decades after the end of the Second World War, some only a year or two afterwards, many more in the early to mid-1950s. For most, the legacy of the war overshadowed their early childhoods even if they didn't realise it at the time. The continuing austerity, the birth of the welfare state, the impact of the war on family life and the change in mood were all significant influences even though, inevitably, some childhoods were affected more than others. What the women said has some similarity to the accounts of authors who have recalled their memories of what it was like to grow up around the 1950s, such as Jacky Hyams in *Bombsites and Lollipops: My 1950s East End Childhood* or Norman Jacobs and his *Pie 'n' Mash & Prefabs: My 1950s Childhood*.

Austerity

Immediately after the war, Britain was still experiencing poverty and unemployment, but it was a nation hoping for a better future. The war had been won, but life was slow to get better as the national debt was at a record high and rationing continued. It was a few years before the post-war economic boom was to get going and the country was to move into what has been termed the Golden Age of the 1950s and 1960s. These better years were described by Harold Macmillan, prime minister at the time, in his famous 1957 speech:

> Let us be frank about it – most of our people have never had it so good. Go around the country, go to the industrial towns, go to the farms and you will see a state of prosperity such as we have never had in my lifetime – nor indeed in the history of this country.

While none of the Sixty Somethings, who grew up to have largely middle-class careers and lives, were among the most deprived of their generation, many talked about the poverty and disarray all around them in their early years. Helen and Margaret mentioned the bomb sites in their neighbourhoods; playing in them but not really taking in that this was where a bomb had fallen not very long before. Many bomb sites, especially in the early 1950s, had become children's playgrounds before they were later cleared, often to make way for National Car Parks before they were sold on for redevelopment. There can be a curious kind of inverted nostalgia for this period of hardship, powerfully evidenced by the huge popularity of the BBC television drama *Call the Midwife*, first broadcast in 2012.

The women commonly talked about growing up under very basic conditions, where money was tight and parents struggled to manage. Frances, for example, recalled how everything was darned and second-hand, and several Sixty Somethings described how their parents would 'make do and mend', many adding that this was something they still do today. Deirdre recalled the regular jumble sales at her school where tables were loaded with a great muddle of cast-off garments, many already on their third life. Skelton's parents had had her at the young ages of 16 and 17 and they 'just worked hard' and 'lived very simple lives'. Theresa remarked how she never had a new bicycle as a child, but that all her own children had had them. Winifred commented how, until she was about 16, it hadn't felt a particularly wonderful time. As she said, there were 'lots of lovely things around me (but) I couldn't afford to be part of them'. Comparing herself with her children, Zena noted how 'my own children had far more in their first five years of life than I had in my whole time at home'. Lois too reported having nothing like the material possessions her children had even though both her parents were GPs. Lynne commented how she never wanted for anything, but she wasn't spoiled.

Even where money was less tight, lives were generally much more frugal than the later experiences of the Sixty Somethings. Chenhalls commented how lives were much more circumscribed but that they didn't see them like that at the time. They were not desperate for the opportunities that subsequently became available to their generation. Lindyloo pointed to the shortage of mod cons, and the greater struggles of everyday life. Among other things, not having a car led her family to shop 'little and often', and little excess money meant her parents didn't bathe more than once a week. This was not atypical. There was hot water only on Fridays in Hayley's household, when her mother lit the boiler or boiled a kettle. The family took it in turns to have baths, the cleanest one first. In Katie's family too, bathing was a weekly event.

Lindyloo talked about it as a 'comfortable but not extravagant existence'. Melissa said her family didn't have the kind of things you would associate with middle-class homes. 'We didn't have books, we didn't have music really, and we didn't have much money because what there was went into the house,' she said. As Meg put it, she and her family led a 'fairly modest, old-fashioned middle-class lifestyle', making do with what you had and learning life skills, such as cooking. Some women did nonetheless recall holidays, even if these were camping, staying with family or going to local resorts.

There were, of course, exceptions, such as Betty's family, who owned their own house and car, or Jo's parents, who never borrowed and never had a mortgage. Maggie's parents had also bought an expensive house, for around £2,000 in 1950, with the consequence that they had a large mortgage and finances were tough.

Quite often family fortunes had changed for the better as the Sixty Somethings were growing up. Helen's family hadn't been very well off when she was very young, but they had later benefited from the success of her maternal grandfather and become able to live in a nice house and pay for her private education. After her grandfather died they became even better off, and were able to lead a 'nice life', going out to restaurants and owning a car. The fortunes of Stella's family also fluctuated, being entirely dependent on what they could earn. They had to be self-dependent as there were no family members to fall back on for financial support. Primrose's circumstances also changed markedly due to her father's employment. When she'd been small, they had been reliant on his low agricultural wage while he tried to be a writer. Later he took a management post with a large retailer that entitled them to live in an 'absolutely enormous beautiful rented house on the banks of the river Thames'.

The National House Condition Survey (now known as the English Housing Survey), was initiated in 1967, and even by this date one in four homes was still without at least one of the basic amenities of a bath or shower, an indoor lavatory, a hand basin, and hot and cold water at three points or more. By 1991, the proportion had dropped to only one in a hundred. Perhaps unsurprisingly, many of the Sixty Somethings described the housing conditions in their family homes as very basic. Hannah, for instance, told of her early life in a big rented house with family and relatives, remembering an electricity socket but nothing to plug into it and only an outside loo (which did flush) and an outside bathroom (which was hardly used). There were electric lights but no hot water unless it had been boiled. She recalls always feeling cold. The family bought a gas fire when she was about ten, but still only one room was ever heated, and a fridge when she was about 11. They didn't acquire a vacuum cleaner before she left home.

Diet was something else the women talked about. Rationing was not finally abolished until 4 July 1954, with bread rationing continuing into 1956, and Barbara remembered meals of carrots, potatoes and cabbage. Food was, at this time, a precious commodity and Sarah told an amusing story about the accidental destruction of a special York ham. This had been a present to her father one Christmas and her mother had decided to cook it in the washing machine. It seems her mistake was not removing it before emptying the water from the machine, as the spin cycle had the unfortunate effect of shredding the ham delicately into the sink.

Despite a restricted diet, the nation was relatively healthy. The Free School Milk Act 1946, entitling all pupils under 18 years to a free third of a pint of milk a day, aided this, as did the nutritional standards set out for school dinners which, according to the Education Act 1944, were to be made available to anyone who wanted them without cost. The third-of-a-pint bottles of free school milk, usually handed out during morning breaks, were a feature of all schoolchildren's lives, only withdrawn from secondary schools in 1968 and for the over-sevens in 1971. Deirdre recalled that, whilst it was generally appreciated, the milk was very unappetising on the occasions it had been left in front of a radiator to defrost.

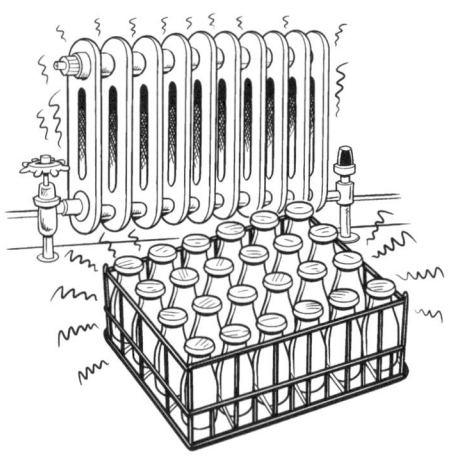

Government advice on growing one's own vegetables and the legacy of the wartime campaign to Dig for Victory, whereby open spaces were turned into allotments and vegetable patches and people were encouraged to grow their own food, were both contributory. Moreover, and according to the RAC's 2007 *Motoring towards 2050 – Roads and Reality* report, only one in five households had access to a car in 1955. This proportion rose to around one in three by 1966 but was still only just above one in two by 1970. Overall there was much greater reliance on walking, cycling and public transport than nowadays. Hayley recalled that, probably as a consequence of lifestyle, most children were healthy and nobody was obese at school.

The women's families

Most of the Sixty Somethings grew up in what might be termed conventional families, usually with natural parents but, in two cases, in adoptive families. The most common number of children in the families of our Sixty Somethings was either two or three. Eight women were only children and the rest were from families of four or more children. The vast majority of siblings were fully biological but a few, especially in the larger reconstructed families, were step- or half-siblings. Although the women didn't routinely indicate the ages of their parents, six specifically mentioned that their fathers were considerably older than their mothers, by twenty years in at least one case. Two also mentioned that their fathers had died when they'd been quite young, four years old in one case and 14 years in the other.

Very few Sixty Somethings were brought up by divorced parents, and nobody said their parents were unmarried. Charlotte commented on how her parents hadn't stayed together but how this had been very unusual. She hadn't known anybody else among her peers in a similar situation. This reflected the times, when the majority of children were born within wedlock and divorce was rare. It did not, however, mean that all marriages were happy, a fact often remarked upon. For many women, growing awareness of their mothers' unhappiness, their emotional and intellectual frustrations, became significant factors in shaping their own choices as adults.

Some Sixty Somethings thought their mothers had felt trapped in their marriages, but that it would have been very difficult for them to leave. Audrey said her mother wouldn't leave her husband because she wasn't prepared to be poor, a point iterated by others too. Many women didn't elaborate on the problems in their parents' marriages, and indeed Patricia indicated it would in any case be difficult to do so. Her parents had a very unhappy relationship and they were very unsuited, but 'it was all kept completely secret so it was difficult to know what the unhappiness was about'. Poppy felt that although her parents were very very happy in the end, their marriage had been more difficult when she'd been growing up. Both she and others suggested their mothers might have been more contented had they had their own lives outside the home to channel some of their interests and energy. Bella remarked that her mother was 'quite bored and lonely a lot of the time, as were a lot of women'. Others offered corroboration, several saying their mothers were clinically depressed, with at least two known to be on tranquillisers. Hayley commented on her parents' marriage, saying that her mother often wanted to leave her father. However, each time she had decided to go, she became pregnant and had to stay.

Poppy described how when her father came home from work he was 'quite happy to have his tea and watch telly', while her mother was more outgoing and wanted 'some bit of life really'. Indeed, many of the everyday family lives of the growing Sixty Somethings were described as quite traditional, with fairly entrenched gender roles. Often women said their fathers did nothing in the domestic line and left housework and childcare largely to their wives. Carol's father's routine, for instance, was to come home for 'dinner' every lunchtime and walk to the pub in the evenings. Her parents rarely went out together. Others suggested that their fathers ruled the roost, particularly if fathers were the only breadwinners and their wives had no independent means. Jacca described her mother as having 'a life imposed on her'. She had no qualifications or financial independence and 'there was no way to break out of that'. Jacca said her father 'could do whatever he liked'. Much the same seemed true in Patricia's family where, as in the 'classic' case, her father gave her 'resentful' mother housekeeping money that she had to survive on. Not all mothers appeared similarly resentful, however. Theresa's mother had also been used to taking orders during the war and didn't seem to mind doing what her husband said. Indeed, her parents were never heard to argue.

Although the traditional pattern seemed most common, some families were different. Poppy's mother, for instance, was a very strong woman who stood up for herself and 'called the shots', and Deirdre considered her parents to have a very equal partnership. Tweegy told how her father was handy around the house when he came back from work, although she's not sure he ever changed a nappy. And although Mary's father never did anything domestic at all, her mother didn't either. The family had au pairs and, thought Mary, were not very typical. Probably also out of the ordinary were Jemima's parents, who regularly dressed for dinner in the evening.

Parents and employment

From what the women said, around two-thirds also grew up in families where the man was the breadwinner and the mother stayed at home to look after the children. Lindyloo is illustrative and said she'd been lucky enough, although she hadn't appreciated it at the time, to have a mother at home who had a hot meal waiting for her. Indeed, the vast majority of women had mothers who did not work, at least while their children were young. As has been noted earlier, in some cases they had given up what appeared to be good jobs, such as radiographer, teacher, actress, ballet dancer, psychiatrist, civil servant or architect. Some went back to work when their children went to school, or to university or, in two cases, when their husbands died. Primrose's mother had in desperation started writing romantic novels because the family was so poor. Fortunately, she had been successful, selling much more than her father, whom Primrose described as a 'failed writer and agricultural worker'. Many, however, did not work again once they had married or had children.

Women's employment was on the up but still not widespread during these years. The female contribution to the workforce during the war was largely lost in peacetime when the jobs women had been doing were 'given back' to the men returning from military service. This policy was supported by the Beveridge Report of 1942 which portrayed the woman's role as in the home with her children, a position reinforced by John Bowlby and his concept of attachment. The belief was that children's long-term well-being depended on the bonds they developed with their mothers. The closure of many nurseries at the end of the war was another factor keeping mothers with small children in the home.

A distinction was, nonetheless, drawn between mothers and single women, and women were barred or sacked from certain occupations during the early 1950s should they be or become married. On the website The Union Makes Us Strong, Mary Davis pointed out in a 2012 article on a history of women at work how despite the availability of jobs for the unmarried, these women were not equal to men in the workplace in terms of pay and benefits. Even the TUC determined in 1949 that equal pay was not appropriate. Some gains for women were made in subsequent years, notably within the civil service and government departments, but marked inequalities remained in the private sector. Opportunities increased for married women over the next years, but female workers were still paid less and faced dismissal if they became pregnant.

Sometimes the mothers of the Sixty Somethings seemed happy not to work. Olive's mother, for example, would never have questioned that her place was in the home, and Tweegy described her mother as 'basically a housewife', saying 'I don't think she resented it.' In other cases the women saw their mothers as frustrated. Lindyloo and Katherine both thought their mothers would have liked a career but both had left school early without qualifications and married husbands who felt it was their role as men to be breadwinners. Hayley, too, thought her mother felt cheated in not having any real paid work after she married. To add insult to injury, she had been told by a social worker that her not working had contributed to difficulties with her other daughter. Betty also said her mother was not a happy housewife. She had a lively mind and would have liked to go out to work. Maggie's mother, who kept hens on a large scale to sell eggs to the Egg Marketing Board and grew vegetables, also seemed to hate being at home. Her daughter said she was 'not sure she felt it was the good life'.

In some cases it seemed that mothers had specific paths they would have liked to have taken. Flavia's mother, for instance, had been a really good pianist but given up the possibility of a musical career to have children. 'I think she really regretted it,' said Flavia. Becoming a doctor and a librarian had been the respective ambitions of Poppy's and Ruby's mothers, neither of which had been achieved. The former had gone to a convent boarding school and left at 16 to work in a bank. These days, suggested Poppy, she would have gone to university, got a degree and had a profession. 'It's very sad; I think she would have thoroughly enjoyed that and it would have channelled some of her energy,' said her daughter. The case of Violet's mother was somewhat different. She had been working in the civil service when she married but had been forced to give up her work. Apparently she had accepted it at the time but later, when she looked back on it, regretted the loss of a job she enjoyed and had been good at.

About one in three mothers of the Sixty Somethings did work while their children were small, although not necessarily in a full-time capacity. Some had professions while others, such as Skelton's mother, 'worked hard to support us but never had a career'. Barbara said her mother worked because she'd grown up in a poor family and was determined her children wouldn't. She'd also been something of a feminist and had felt it was her right to work, even if it did result in some feelings of guilt. The jobs and professions of these mothers included clerical work, managing a shop, secretary, taking in paying guests, youth worker, cleaner, civil servant, GP, teacher and company secretary. Hazel Grace's mother worked for a film company as a story editor. She was watching a play when she went into labour but insisted on completing and filing her report before going to hospital to give birth. A few other mothers acted as assistants to their husbands who were doctors or farmers or, in the case of Stella, co-ran a nightclub. Some, such as Meg's mother, who was involved in public life as a councillor, had unpaid occupations that took them out of the home. Beth said her mother did some voluntary work for the Citizens Advice Bureau, but, 'I don't think she did anything much.' Apparently, she wrote a lot of letters to relatives but couldn't really be called a housewife as she employed paid staff.

Fathers, by contrast, were expected to work and were doing so. Nobody mentioned that their father had been unemployed, although several listed more than one type of occupation or career they had been employed in. As already noted, there was much less social mobility between the Sixty Somethings and their parents than there had been between their parents and grandparents. As a result, almost all the women grew up in homes that could broadly be described as middle class. Fathers overall were employed in a wide range of occupations across the social spectrum, although few seemed to have taken very low-paid manual occupations. The professional jobs mentioned included GPs, surgeon, civil servants, solicitor, university lecturer, journalist, novelist, politician, teacher, headmaster, a variety of engineering specialities, quantity surveyor, barrister, agronomist and architect. Others were employed by the local authority, managed shops or worked as farmer, publican, mechanic, postman, storeman, sub-postmaster, wedding photographer, aircraft rigger, window cleaner, shopkeeper, factory worker or fireman. Some ran their own businesses, whether in printing, haulage, wood-turning, entertainment or retail.

Interestingly, a number of fathers had occupations with international links. Jacca's father had been an architect designing oil pipelines in the Middle East, Clara's worked for an office supplies firm in Zimbabwe (called Rhodesia at the time), Julia's father was in the Indian political service in the British Raj and Molly's father moved from being a junior officer in the Indian army to a major in the military police in Cyprus. Violet's father worked for a firm dealing with gold mines and diamond mines in South Africa, while Zena's father was a crane driver working overseas on 18-month to two-year contracts and therefore away a lot. He returned to work nearer home when she was about ten. Ruby's father, a refugee from Nazi Germany, had a summer job as a courier for tour groups around Europe, although he was a journalist, translator and teacher at other times. He had at one time had the job of translating Hitler's speeches. Meg's father didn't work abroad but, as a vet, covered a large rural area of the country. 'If it was nice weather in summer, we'd just go with him and sit on the beach. It was idyllic,' she said.

Many Sixty Somethings were impressed by their fathers' work ethic. Persia told how her father had worked his way to the top since leaving school at 14. Melissa told how hers, a construction engineer, 'kept moving because he was always trying to go another step up the ladder'. She saw work as a key part of his life. Jan's father too, a GP who had come to England from Scotland, had a strong work ethic and 'didn't have much time for anyone who had airs and graces', even though he did like 'the nicer things in life when he was able to afford them'. Only one criticised a parent for being 'lazy'.

Families getting on

Many of the women talked about their relationships with their parents, which became models for their own parenting. Many were positive, to be emulated, while others were negative and to be avoided. For some there were only happy memories. Betty considered she'd had a 'very secure, stable sort of upbringing' with 'really lovely' parents who were very flexible and outward-looking. There had been boundaries but they weren't heavy boundaries. Clara too was very positive about her parents, saying 'I adored them completely.' She remembered a feeling of family and participation and togetherness. Deirdre said she had fond memories of her childhood and 'no complaints of any kind' about her parents, while Jo recalled her father as 'very jolly and good fun in lots of ways' but didn't think she'd been brought up by conventional parents. Hayley too told of a great upbringing in the sense that there were always family poems on the go alongside painting, books and live music. Many parents also did much to instil values in their children and provide them with formative experiences. Ruby, for instance, told how she had been brought up to question authority, while Primrose's first instance of protest was being taken on a CND march by her 'radical, feminist' parents.

Many women, nonetheless, talked of a certain distance between themselves and their parents, contrasting how they'd been brought up with how they'd parented their own children. Zena suggested that her parents and their generation saw children as appendages, while Poppy summed up the view of many in saying that while her parents 'totally loved us all', they weren't as child-centred as she and her generation had been. Helen enlarged on this point, telling how her father didn't do much with the children, although they did create a bond through the books he would give her, and her mother was always occupied with a 'mass of housework'. Maggie felt her mother wasn't the warmest of mothers, 'not a cuddly mother', but she still did right by her children. Winifred commented how 'it would never have occurred to my mother to play with me' or to hug her children, read them stories or take them places. She thought her own generation was 'in the middle between two extremes', mothers still influenced by the reserve of the Victorian era and the liberated post-war group. Lois too had few memories of doing much with her mother and, after her parents divorced, felt her remarried father had little interest in her or her siblings.

The difficulty with expressing emotion recalled by a number of women was very touchingly illustrated by Norah. A few moments before her father died at the age of 77, he had told her 'I love you' for the first time ever. She said she'd always known that he did, but it was just not something her parents ever said. This lack of overt emotional reaction extended to when she'd received her A-level results. At the time Norah's father had been quite non-committal and it was only when she talked to somebody he played bowls with that she'd learned how proud of her he'd been. He hadn't been able to tell her himself.

Unsurprisingly, relationships tended to be closer with mothers than fathers, who not only were more often away because of work but who also may not have seen it as their role to look after the children, instead pursuing their own activities such as playing golf or going to the pub. Moreover, it seemed likely that relationships could be affected by earlier formative experiences. Maureen suggested, for instance, that fathers who had come back from war often bottled things up and didn't want to talk. It seemed there could be a disjuncture between the generations, as in Jenny's family. She felt the war had been a deeply traumatic time for her father. 'Dad used to thump me all the time, but I'm sure it was PTSD from the war. He was in Burma fighting the Japs and had terrible nightmares. I used to think it was funny because I didn't understand it.' In her view, 'he must have been a good chap at one point and then the war knackered him.' Other Sixty Somethings thought that their fathers' unhappy childhoods and poor relationships with their own parents had taken an emotional toll. This applied to Maggie's father, who had been 'a very silent man' and played little part in family life, as well as to Audrey's father who was said to be 'a truly difficult person'. Sometimes, too, fathers were said to be depressed, unwell or battling with problems such as alcoholism or diabetes. In Primrose's case, and for whatever reason, she thought her father just found it difficult to deal with family life.

Some, but by no means all, Sixty Somethings regarded their upbringing as fairly strict. Flavia was one who thought that in her day 'a lot of women were very strictly brought up and have been struggling with very low self-confidence because of that.' She thought communication was very difficult between the generations, much more so than nowadays, and said many of her friends agreed. Jan said this was true of her family and Lindyloo commented that you had to 'know your place'. Poppy remembered being made to eat everything on her plate and how Sunday dinners were a nightmare as she couldn't stand fatty meat. She said she would be sitting at the table through *Desert Island Discs*, the *Billy Cotton Band Show* and the *Navy Lark* with the uneaten food in front of her.

Several women also talked about the risk of physical punishment. Maggie recalled the threat of 'when your father comes home' and remembered being sent to his study, put over his knee and spanked. Tweegy was also told that 'your father will speak to you when he gets home'. Apparently he never lost his temper but he would express his disappointment, which she found hard to bear. Melissa regarded herself as the 'black sheep of the family' and, although she hadn't remembered herself, had been told by her sister that their mother had confessed to 'clouting' her quite a bit when she was little. Elizabeth's family was also quite strict but she thought that was due to her particular parents rather than necessarily the times. Indeed, it seemed to be the minority of women who had grown up under stricture, or at least recalled such an upbringing.

Whether or not they were close, it seemed there were often difficulties of communication within families, especially around sensitive topics. Many women talked about difficulties in discussing sex with their parents. A common taboo for some was talking about 'the facts of life', especially menstruation. When Katie's mother nervously tried to introduce the topic, Katie lied and said she already knew, to her mother's evident relief. Like many children of this generation, she says, she picked up fragmentary and sometimes inaccurate information from friends.

Flavia's first period took her by surprise as nobody had told her anything about it. Her mother had found the subject difficult to broach and later tried to explain it by talking about their dog being on heat, adding that her older sister was sometimes affected too. Flavia said she'd then asked, 'Does that mean she can't see boys for a week or so?' Norah also said her parents 'didn't name things directly'. She tells of getting a letter from her mother after she'd left home to say that she'd be interested to know that her sister is now a woman. She had started her periods. On the other hand, Barbara talked about her mother as quite prudish in some ways but liberated in others. She'd told her the facts of life at a young age in a quite unembarrassed way, but later got very flustered when Barbara asked her about masturbation. Her response was to tell her to go and look it up.

In this climate it is perhaps unsurprising that teenage births were on the rise during the 1950s and 1960s. The Office for National Statistics reveal how they increased from a rate of 23.5 per thousand women aged 15 to 19 years in 1955 to 49.6 per thousand in 1969. Nonetheless, both sex and the possibility of pregnancy were strongly frowned upon by many parents. Melissa said promiscuous behaviour was forbidden and Eleanor, Jemima, Lynne and Patricia were among those to say they would have been thrown out and disowned had they become pregnant. Indeed, one woman said her sister had been banished by her parents after being caught in bed with her boyfriend. Barbara also talked about a girl at school who got pregnant at 15 or 16 and was never heard of again. Such were parents' concerns that Katherine, aged only seven or eight, was enlisted as a chaperone for her much older sister, 'who used to hang around Brize Norton where all the American guys were'. Katherine spent her time sitting in coffee bars, with soldiers patting her on the head and buying her biscuits.

One, who had a pregnancy scare in her late teens, said she would never have dreamed of telling her mother about it, let alone her father. Another, who did become pregnant, said her mother was fine about it but her father wanted her to have an abortion. He felt her pregnancy reflected on him and he couldn't show her off in the same way any more. It had hit him the hardest.

The lack of communication in some families reached a peak for Hayley, whose mother suffered from mental health problems and spent periods of time in hospital. On one occasion, when Hayley was six or seven years old, she had not been given a reason for her mother's absence and assumed she had died. She was then very surprised when her mother turned up three months later.

More generally, it seemed that poor intergenerational communication could go in both directions. Dolly reflected how 'we didn't understand our parents and you're not supposed to', while Elizabeth thought 'our lives were a mystery to our parents'.

The role of religion in early lives

Religion can play a variety of roles in people's lives. It can be a label and identity, it can be a belief system, it can be a practice or behaviour, or it can revolve around a sense of community or belonging. Moreover, it can be some or all of these things at any one time. The Sixty Somethings' recollections of their childhoods display this complexity of religion in their early lives. As discussed in Chapter 7, churchgoing and professing a religious identity were more common at that date than currently.

About three-quarters of the women who provided information suggested that religion was important to some degree as they were growing up. All these tended to give themselves a religious label, even if they didn't provide much additional information. Thus they may have said they were christened or confirmed within the Church of England, born into a Catholic family, or brought up as Baptist, Presbyterian or in the Quaker tradition. More unusually, Jenny was brought up as Methodist to start with but then became Church of England as her mother aspired to the middle classes.

Although some Sixty Somethings suggested religion had been important to them and their families at that time, there were others who indicated it was not a critical aspect of their identity. Audrey, for instance, said hers was not a particularly religious family, despite her father coming from a long line of clergy, and Bella thought she had been christened into the Church of England more because of family pressures than parental beliefs. She recalled going to Brownies, although only for one week. 'It wasn't really my scene,' she said. She was taught how to lay tables but was interested in more adventurous activities.

Others, such as Olive and Primrose, suggested their families were involved in religion as an institution and were not sure how much it actually meant to them. Religion as a customary practice was illustrated by Geraldine, who said her family went to church at Christmas and Easter 'like everyone else' and that 'we were all C of E'. However, it meant 'everything and nothing'. Religion permeated all their institutions and they knew all the hymns in the hymn book, even if its deeper meaning wasn't clear. Katie and her younger brother were taken to Church of England services by her mother every other Sunday. Years later her mother admitted that she had lost her faith while at university but thought that churchgoing was important for her children's 'moral education'.

It is not unusual for people to have strong feelings about religion during their teenage years, as Nicola Madge and colleagues have shown in *Youth on Religion*, a 2014 report on a large study of religiosity among secondary school pupils living in culturally diverse areas of Britain. Indeed, three Sixty Somethings described what might be termed conversion experiences at this time. Audrey remembered how the 'scales fell from my eyes' when she was about 14 or 15 years old, and how she realised 'how massively manipulative it all was'. She reasoned that it is fine to have no religion in a world that values different religions and so became an atheist. Helen had a similar experience during her teenage years. She described thinking about religion and coming to the conclusion that it was 'a load of hokum'. Melissa too said she'd had a 'crisis' at 16 years and left the church.

Katherine also had an intense religious experience during her teenage years, but this took a different direction. In her case she became strongly religious, partly as a reaction against her mother. She said she rebelled against her family by going to church, rather than the more typical other way round. She said it gave her an alternative family and blended very well with her socialist views. She learned about social responsibility and at 15 years had gone on a silent march in support of Martin Luther King. She felt it was a move away from the repressive viewpoint of the 1950s that brought children up to believe they were sinners.

Some Sixty Somethings were religious bystanders in the sense that religion had never played an important role in their lives. Alison, for instance, had some experience of religion through events such as weddings and christenings and by joining the equivalent of Scottish Brownies but had not been brought up as religious. Her father had told her that if she wanted to be christened later, she could do it herself. Lindyloo had also been brought up to make her own decisions. She described her mother as having some belief but not practising, but said that her father had gone through the war and, as a result, thought that God could not exist.

A few women came from families strongly opposed to religion. Lynne said she had grown up in a family that thought that religion was the cause of wars and unrest and that her parents were completely secular and had no belief in God. She said they still helped people and thought that 'Christianity stopped you doing that'. Beth's father described himself as a 'fundamentalist agnostic', and Liza's family hadn't gone to church for generations. Several others came from families that did not practise religion in any form and perhaps labelled themselves as atheist. In one of these, and atypically, Maggie had tried to convert her parents to Christianity as a teenager.

Three women came from Jewish families and illustrated well how identity can be more to do with race and a sense of community than a matter of faith. Neither of Ruby's parents, both of whom came to Britain from Germany, had been brought up to observe Jewish teaching. While her mother was raised as a Lutheran Christian, her father had grown up feeling that being a Jew was part of his identity and community even though he had not been religiously observant. After the Second World War, however, when many family members were lost, he wanted to become more Jewish and so the family as a whole became more observant, celebrating the main festivals. Rachel's parents hadn't had the same experiences but had a strong sense of identity with the Jewish community. They mixed only with Jewish people, and home life was circumscribed and organised around the synagogue and celebrated festivals.

Freedom and restrictions

Even if some Sixty Somethings were brought up quite strictly, they frequently spoke of the freedom and independence they were given to go out and entertain themselves, often for long hours and far from parental surveillance. The 1950s indeed were seen as a time of more permissive parenting compared to the earlier years when 'experts' such as Truby King had advocated the importance of rigid timetabling of mealtimes and limited affection. The popularity of Dr Benjamin Spock and his widely read *The Common Sense Book of Baby and Child Care*, published in 1946, had set a new tone. The essence of this prescription, reinforced by Donald Winnicott the year before in *Getting to Know Your Baby*, was to follow your instincts and trust your children to be sensible. Winnicott told parents to aspire to being 'good enough' rather than perfect.

Many women talked about the freedom they experienced growing up and how they were allowed out on the streets and parks, could travel to school on their own and were generally encouraged to be independent. There were bobbies on the beat, park keepers were still employed to keep an eye out and, according to Zena, there was much more community responsibility for children. As Eleanor said, parents didn't worry too much. Sylvie elaborated by recounting her wonderful childhood where she was free to do what she wanted – cycling, swimming, rescuing kittens, watching calves being born – and nobody was concerned about paedophiles or traffic. She told of near-death experiences her parents never found out about. Once she got stuck halfway up a cliff with a huge boulder towering over her, and on another occasion she nearly drowned when she was swimming in the sea and fell in a hole. She also told a story about a girl who fell off a jetty and was being swept away up the Mersey. She would have drowned if two boys in a fishing boat hadn't managed to rescue her. When she got home her mother had asked her how she'd got so wet and she just said she fell in a rock pool.

At the same time, however, many women had felt uncomfortably restricted at home. Lindyloo was not allowed to go to the coffee bar and knew it was 'naughty' to listen to Radio Luxembourg under the bedcovers, and Winifred said she got hit a lot, for offences such as getting dirty. Miranda felt repressed and was not allowed to play pop music, Stella was discouraged from reading the *Jackie* comic because of its bad influence, and Alison said her mother was concerned about her going near 'sleazy shops' in London. It seemed many parents were concerned about what the neighbours might think, or were conscious of their status. Maureen, for instance, was not allowed to walk through the council estate on her way to school even though it was by far the quickest route. And Katherine told how, when she was 13 going on 14, she wasn't allowed to wear jeans because they were common. She'd been told the family was 'working class, but we have our standards'. As she said, all she wanted to do was hang around the jukebox wearing sloppy joes. She felt her parents thought she was a lost cause.

There seemed to be a resignation on the part of some women that, in the end, it was simplest to do what was expected of them. Dolly said she used to wear incredibly short skirts but that, other than that, 'you were a nice middle-class girl and you did what you were told. Or you did what was expected.' And Alice said, 'My mother was very old-fashioned in her expectations and I did what she said always because I didn't want to offend or upset or worry her.' Molly had tried rebelling at the age of five, when she couldn't understand why a boy she was friendly with could play only in her garden and not her house (it transpired that his father was not considered sufficiently high-status) and kicked out at that. But the pressures were too great, and 'so I kicked at various points but I always got back in the box again.' Lindyloo said she never really discussed anything with her parents but just did what she was told. For Norah, the message from her father was that something was right if he said it was.

Not all, however, felt constrained. Charlotte admitted to always mixing with 'the naughty group' at school. She didn't mind that they all smoked and she stuck by them even though she didn't smoke herself and still got punished. Betty said they knew the boundaries, but her mother was always encouraging her children to think they were doing something a bit naughty. Betty thought it a good strategy and tried to do it with her own children.

The freedom they had was, for many of the women, their salvation as, according to Zena, 'Life was pretty boring so you had to provide your own interests.' She said she could list all the pubs she and her brother stood outside with their R Whites and crisps. 'We never went anywhere else,' she said. Theresa also told how there wasn't much to do and that, as teenagers, she and friends would go to the pub and make half a pint last a very long time.

The possibilities for entertainment were indeed limited. Going out for a meal was not something young people did, as the Sixty Somethings reported, and was in any case expensive. Youth clubs existed, often aligned to the church, but weren't always where young people wanted to go. Most towns had cinemas, but their popularity was in decline. David Docherty and colleagues record in their 1987 book *The Last Picture Show? Britain's Changing Film Audiences* how attendance was at its peak in the immediate post-war period, but that audience figures then dropped by 70 per cent between 1946 and 1960 as television was gradually introduced into homes during the 1950s. Indeed, Broadcasters' Audience Research Board figures show that while around one in three UK households had television at the beginning of the 1950s, this proportion had doubled by the beginning of the 1960s. Bella had been one of the lucky ones. Her parents were reasonably comfortable financially and they got a television when she was about twelve. She remembered it as a big box with a tiny screen.

There were, however, only limited programmes specifically for children, with only a single channel until the launch of ITV, the first commercial channel, in 1955. *Watch with Mother* and *Children's Hour* were for several years really the only offerings. Puppets like Andy Pandy, Bill and Ben and the Woodentops became the icons of early childhood. Many Sixty Somethings can still sing the theme songs of *Robin Hood* and *The Adventures of William Tell*, while *The Lone Ranger* shared the 'William Tell Overture', but speeded up. Viewing was also restricted to certain hours with, until 1957, a period of one hour, between 6 p.m. and 7 p.m., known as the 'toddlers' truce', when no programmes were broadcast in the hope that young children would think television was finished for the day and go to bed without protest.

Most families had a radio, still commonly called 'the wireless', and from 1954 *Children's Favourites* on the Light Programme with 'Uncle Mac' became a Saturday morning fixture in many households, immortalising songs like 'Nellie the Elephant', 'The Runaway Train' and 'The Laughing Policeman'. One of Deirdre's early memories was standing on a stool in front of the large family Murphy wireless, eating a toasted ham sandwich and listening to the coronation of Elizabeth II.

Schooling

The Education Act 1944 radically changed the education system in England and Wales through the introduction of a tripartite secondary system of grammar, technical and secondary modern schools, and by extending free education to all state secondary schools. The heyday of the grammar school was ushered in. Figures from a 2017 briefing paper by the House of Commons Library show how the proportion of secondary pupils attending these schools peaked at almost 38 per cent in 1947, with the absolute numbers of grammar schools and their pupils at their highest of 1,300 and 726,000 respectively in 1964. After that, numbers began to decline markedly, especially after 1965, when the new Labour government instructed local authorities to begin converting all schools to comprehensives. The proportion of pupils in grammar schools is nowadays below 5 per cent.

It was not always completely clear what kinds of school the Sixty Somethings went to. However, it seems that up to a quarter went to a grammar school of some sort at secondary level. Nine went to a boarding school for at least part of their education, six mentioned religious schools, six mentioned private schools, four had moved around a lot and attended schools abroad as well as in Britain, three mentioned comprehensives and one a secondary modern. Most had attended more than one school. The majority left at 18 but three said they had left at 16.

Many of the women who talked about their education said how excellent it had been. It was a formative experience and an important start to their lives. Lilian claimed that 'access to education made us the women we are today', and Violet was among those to say how education had been improving when she was at school. Julia pointed out that she and her peers weren't subject to the experiments in education children nowadays experience every time there is a new government. She said there was more stability and continuity than these days. Hayley thought that the education included being 'brought up to be well-behaved', recalling being rapped on the knuckles and having to stand on a chair because she got her nine times table wrong. However, she was not reproving. She wasn't sure that the discipline was 'stifling creativity' as 'a lot of major changes were instigated by people brought up strictly'.

Several women attested to the positive way schools encouraged freethinking and questioning. Education was about getting you to think rather than just filling your head with information. Meg said challenging authority became a reflex and Persia said education had made her generation believe you could achieve things. This is well illustrated by Verity's memory of sitting with friends in the garden of her school in the sixth form discussing what they would be doing in ten years' time. Nobody mentioned husbands or children. Once they had been to university, the world would be their oyster and they would be able to do whatever they wanted. They had no specific plans or careers in mind. It was just that they were all confident they would be successful.

University was of course important for success and, as Chenhalls said, a grammar school education was an important stepping stone in that direction. Moreover, grammar schools at that time could also be social levellers. According to Sylvie, her grammar school was 'full of daughters of charladies and shop assistants ... a very inclusive place ... that allowed for so much energy to come through'. However, this didn't seem to have been everybody's perception. Lilian recalled a fellow pupil, one of the 'bright kids', who was hoping to go to grammar school but wasn't allowed to. Her parents said she was going to work in the mill. Lilian said, 'It's something that's stayed with me all my life. But her parents didn't see her as someone who would go to grammar school.'

It would be surprising if everyone had fond memories of school, and of course they didn't. Two women said they had been expelled and one said she had tried to run away from school. There were also specific criticisms. Most commonly mentioned was the very limited careers advice on offer. Elizabeth didn't feel a great deal was expected, and suggestions were along the lines of 'go to M&S'. In Lindyloo's experience, the recommended choice was usually between teacher training, university or insurance. For Theresa it seemed to be between nursing or teaching or going to university. Another criticism was that sex education was negligible. According to Katherine, sex was very much a whispered thing and she and her friends had many unanswered questions. A third criticism, although mentioned only by two women, was the inequality observed between the sexes, even at an early age. Eleanor recollects that boys were allowed out later and permitted to do things the girls couldn't at her mixed primary school. Sarah's story was that she felt hopeless at cookery at school and asked if she could do woodwork with the boys. There was a bit of a 'hoo-ha' and she was told not to be ridiculous.

Parents' expectations for their daughters

Universities were experiencing a period of enormous expansion just at the time the Sixty Somethings were leaving school and thinking about the possibility of higher education. Information compiled by the House of Commons Library in 2012 showed that whereas the total number of students gaining university degrees in the UK was 17,337 in 1950, this had risen to 22,426 in 1960 and 51,189 in 1970. Nonetheless, even at this latter date participation in higher education was only at 8.4 per cent of the population, compared with a present-day rate of between 40 and 50 per cent. As shown later, the Sixty Somethings were atypical of their age group as a whole in that the majority of them achieved a degree at some stage in their life.

What support did these women get from their parents in pursuing education and a career? There was no single pattern and very varying levels of encouragement. Some parents had low expectations, while others were aspirational for their daughters. Sometimes parents were keen for them to have the advantages they had never had themselves.

A considerable number of women said their parents retained a traditional outlook and did not expect them to be high achievers. They wanted their children to be happy but didn't expect them to have careers. Typically, Alice was told it didn't matter what she did because she would probably get married, while Alison thought her parents just wanted her to be happy and have a nice man to look after her. Zena said her mother wanted her to do well, but that's as far as it went. 'I think she'd have liked me to move round the corner, become a secretary, and go back to her for Sunday lunch all the time.' Very similar comments were made by many others and, as Annie said, there was a feeling that their parents' generation didn't expect their daughters to have careers. Jenny said her parents thought she'd have done well if she got a job at Woolworths. They were happy enough when she became a teacher but when she got a degree her mother said, 'What's that and why have you wasted three years of your life doing that?' She couldn't see the point when Jenny was already a teacher. And she thought she was 'completely barking bonkers' when she went on to do a master's degree at 40.

Clara, who didn't go to university but would have liked to, said her mother's generation, at her level of social strata, would all be housewives. Her father had been to university, 'but you didn't send your girls to university ... We went to secretarial college so we could become independent ... and we were going to meet a lovely, kind young man with a pot of money, get married and live happily ever after. That was probably their dream. But neither my sister nor I have ended up like that.' Dolly didn't go to university either and, coming from a very 'traditional' family, said there was no expectation that she would do so or have a career. Her parents never thought she would carry on working once she was married and had a family, and she wondered what her father would have said had he known she was now a WASPI woman (see later) who would have to go on working until she was 66.

Some women made it to higher education despite their parents' opposition, or at least without their express enthusiasm. For Flavia it had been 'a big deal' for her parents that she passed the eleven-plus, but they didn't want her to go to university. It took her school to persuade them to let her apply, but even then they said, 'Okay but it's got to be London.' She ended up going to a university in the north of the country. Theresa said her father's comment when she told him she was giving up her job to go on teacher training was 'Why can't you just marry a rich Catholic solicitor?' 'Even if I get married, Dad, I'll still go on working,' she had replied. Minnie's mother had never approved of her having a career, especially when she continued to do so after having children.

By way of contrast, many women such as Annie said their parents wanted them to get a good education and take advantage of opportunities they hadn't had themselves. Molly is a good example, saying there was no question in her family that she wasn't going to university, and indeed that her parents even 'kindly decided what degree I'd do … It was a good choice because I was suited to that career, but it wasn't my choice of career.' In both her case and that of her partner, she thought 'parents were projecting what they hadn't had on to their children'. Lindyloo, too, said she always felt her father wanted his children to do better than he had. He had got books to help her pass the eleven-plus and she was brought up to have aspiration and ambition.

Many other parents, too, encouraged their children to pursue their education and have careers. Verity said, 'One of the happiest things for my mother was when I was 14 ... and she was told I was university material. All her friends' children had gone to university. It was the norm.' Sometimes they suggested higher goals than their daughters had first thought of. Barbara's own initial expectations had been to become a teacher but her parents encouraged her to set her goal at university lecturer. Earlier, when she'd been about ten, she'd wanted to be a doctor. Her parents had never told her she should be a nurse. Equally, Tweegy had wanted to be a nurse but was encouraged by her parents, and a female GP role model, to become a doctor.

Fathers sometimes seemed to be the most active supporters of their daughters' education. In Lynne's case, it was her father's priority to get her educated, even though she was a girl. He was determined she should go as far as possible given her intellectual capacity and helped her choose her profession. Melissa also recalled her father pushing her educationally, and Ruby told how her father was very keen on education for both her and her brothers, spending all his spare money on supporting them. Norah's father too had been influential in determining her educational pathway, and it was he who suggested the university she should apply to. Apparently the idea came from an episode of *University Challenge* the previous year when one of the members of the institution in question said, by way of introduction, 'I'm reading spasmodically.' This had appealed to them and 'It seemed like a good place to go.'

Sometimes, of course, mothers could be as forceful as fathers. Meg's parents didn't have sexist ideas, and she and her siblings were all going to university. So when Meg once suggested an alternative path to her mother – cooking – she was immediately told 'no, you're not'. 'You just didn't argue and I knew basically that she was right.'

Perhaps reflecting the times, many women suggested there had been greater support for their brothers and male peers than there had been for them when it came to going to university and getting degrees. In 1960 there were three times as many men as women gaining first degrees, and there were still more than twice as many by 1970. It wasn't until the massive expansion in the 1990s that women overtook men, a position they have maintained to this day.

Barbara said her mother talked with pride about her son in a way she didn't about her daughter, and Carol, Geraldine, Julia, Olive, Poppy, Rachel and Violet were among those who agreed that expectations were generally greater for males than females even if parents were pleased when their daughters did well. Barbara said that although her father was very supportive of her academically, she always felt he would have preferred it if her brother had been the academically successful one. Applying for a prestigious university, she remembers lying awake at night feeling absolutely furious that only 1 in 10 places went to women. When she got there she found a lot of 'dim public-school boys' but not other 'bright women' who had also applied. She came to despise men who were against colleges admitting women and who, to her mind, were saying 'there's 50 per cent of the human race that we don't want to teach because they don't have the dangly bits'. Minnie also thought it pained her father that she was brighter than her brother, and Lois expected her mother was disappointed when she got a place at university but her brother didn't.

All the same, by no means all Sixty Somethings felt at a disadvantage compared to their brothers or other young men of their age. Audrey, Elizabeth, Frances, Jan, Flavia, Persia, Robin, Stephanie and Tweegy were among those to make this point. For Bella, as a woman with a strict Victorian father, 'the attitude was you can do whatever you want to do so long as you are prepared to work for it.'

Of course, parents might not always agree with one another, and whereas Lynne's father was keen for her to get a good education, her mother would probably have preferred her living round the corner as the girl next door. Sometimes one parent might be more involved than the other. Thus for Alice her father's views were mainly mediated through her mother, and while Jacca's father suggested she might become a secretary or join the Forces when she left school, her mother didn't have a view. There could also be intergenerational disagreement. Chenhalls's parents strongly encouraged her to go to university, but her grandparents were certainly not in favour.

As it transpired, most of the Sixty Somethings did go on to university or some other type of training, either sooner or later. For many this signalled a stark culture shock as well as profound changes in attitudes and behaviours. Their thoughts and experiences during this next phase of their lives are explored in the following chapter.

4

Talking About My Generation

It was the latter half of the sixties and into the early seventies when the Sixty Somethings were leaving school and moving on to the next stage of their lives. For most this meant leaving home, usually to go to university or some other form of professional training, and often for good. Once away from their families many became exposed to very different cultures involving sex, drugs and rock 'n' roll – even if some had prior knowledge in these areas. This section examines their views and experiences, and the choices they made about their own lifestyles and identities as they progressed through their teenage years and into early adulthood. It also looks at whether or not these women, who were certainly not typical of their age group as a whole, might be regarded as part of a 'hippy' generation who embraced the 'alternative' lifestyles that followed.

She's leaving home

University expansion had been gradually increasing since the war, but it was the 1960s that saw the most dramatic increase to date. With the introduction of what have been termed the 'new universities', such as East Anglia, Essex, Kent, Sussex and York, the number of universities went up from 22 to 45 and overall participation in higher education increased from 3.4 per cent in 1950 to 8.4 per cent in 1970. It then remained stable until the next wave of expansion in the 1980s. The image of these new universities went beyond education and projected an aura of glamour. Modern in their architecture, and often set in green parklands, they could suggest a new kind of utopia. In the last episode of his landmark television series *Civilisation* (1969), the grand art historian Kenneth Clark heralded the concrete ziggurats of the campus of the University of East Anglia as the nursery of a new cultured democracy.

These new 'plate glass universities' were also frequently presented as lifestyle choices. This is illustrated by Catherine and Helen, the Jay Twins, who studied at Sussex University between 1963 and 1966. Epitomising everything that was desirable, with their good looks and privileged backgrounds, these sisters were portrayed in the Sunday colour supplements and other widely circulated publications. There was a clear message. University was not at all dull and stuffy. It was an exciting place to be.

A disproportionate number of women in the sample followed the trend, whatever their personal reason, into higher education even if this was without particular support from their families. Of the women, 41 went straight, or almost straight, to university from school, 8 enrolled in teacher training (with 3 of these completing a degree at a later date), 5 went into nursing (with 3 gaining a later degree), 2 went to drama school (one gaining a degree much later), 1 went to art college (later gaining a teaching degree) and 5 undertook degrees at a later stage. Only five did not pursue any form of higher education.

Very often, these women were the first in their families to go to university. As several said, it represented a considerable unknown for both themselves and their parents, who probably didn't know anybody with a degree. Minnie's mother didn't know what university was, never mind what it did. As far as she was concerned, they were 'communist places where you learned to "sit in" and do nothing'. She assumed Minnie would marry and stay at home, offering little approval of her career, especially when she continued to work after her children were born. Stella also pointed out how university was the unknown, even to teachers, who had rarely been to university themselves. In her view, everybody was working on the basis of non-information. Only one person from her very large extended family had been to university, and everyone said 'he was weird anyway'. Indeed, her mother had told her 'No way. You're not going to university!', and she hadn't.

A lack of specific knowledge didn't put the women off. Many of the Sixty Somethings saw leaving home and abandoning what they regarded as the strictures and prejudices of their parents as a priority. Jenny, for instance, said she left home 'with skates on' to go to teacher training college when she was 18, Tabitha said 'I left home the minute I could at 17 and never went back' and Skelton told how she couldn't wait to leave home. Many others too never went back again afterwards, and several described how they or their friends of a similar age from northern and rural areas made a determined move to London at that point. Londoner Ruby, for instance, went up North rather than return home after she'd completed her degree. Her father expected her 'to stay at home until I married and so I had to do something to get away from home'. Nonetheless, she 'nearly died of loneliness' after six months and had to go back to London, albeit not to her family home. For many, going away effectively brought their parents' child-rearing phase to an end. Some, like Helen, said their families knew little about their lives from that point onwards.

Even if they didn't know exactly what to expect, the women had their own expectations of the education or training they wanted to pursue. Sometimes they focused on a specific career, but often their concern was to broaden their minds and use their brains. Some contrasted their attitudes at the time with those of young people these days. Confident of finding the jobs they wanted, they'd been less likely to see university as a meal ticket.

Education or training wasn't the only destination for the young women keen to leave home as soon as they could. Katherine had been told that if you could support yourself when you were 17, you could leave home and nobody would stop you. Accordingly, on her seventeenth birthday, she gave notice to her family and school and was off. She went to London, got a job and got married. Jo 'ran away' from school to live with a boyfriend instead.

Let's spend the night together

The sexual revolution, typified by the challenge to traditional sexual norms and greater acceptance of sex outside marriage, is generally assumed to date from the sixties and extend into the seventies and eighties, a view enshrined in Philip Larkin's 1967 poem 'Annus Mirabilis' which begins 'Sexual intercourse began / In nineteen sixty-three…' Of course, there is ample evidence that sexual promiscuity was not uncommon before that time, and that sex was certainly not invented in the sixties. Countless earlier biographies, and too many to detail, tell of *liaisons dangereuses*, infidelities and sexual shenanigans since time began. And, unsurprisingly, behaviours did not suddenly change. Katie's brother told her of a female colleague who had been at university in the 1950s and claimed she slept with a different man almost every night. 'I chewed them up and spat them out.'

Nevertheless, the so-called sexual revolution coincided with the time when many of the Sixty Somethings had entered higher education or professional training and were living away from home with opportunities for sexual experimentation. What were their memories of the time?

Unsurprisingly, the Pill, which came just at the 'right' time for most of the Sixty Somethings, was mentioned by almost everyone and heralded as a 'huge watershed', 'very liberating', and making 'a most massive difference'. It was 1961 when it became available in Great Britain through the NHS at the subsidised price of two shillings a month. At this time it was largely prescribed for married women who didn't want any more children, and it took several years, until 1967, for it to be made available to married and unmarried women alike. This policy change, according to Kaye Wellings and colleagues, who published *Sexual Behaviour in Britain: The National Survey of Sexual Attitudes and Lifestyles* in 1986, was reflected in its increased take-up from an estimated 50,000 to about a million women in Great Britain between 1962 and 1969. By 1974, family planning clinics could prescribe the Pill, at no cost, to all women.

According to Winifred, 'it was handed to us on a plate … And obviously, who wouldn't? We went along with it because we could.' Indeed, the majority of the women spoke openly about how 'the sexual slackening off was second nature' and how 'it was all happening'. A number of women said they had been very 'permissive' or 'promiscuous'. Verity was not atypical in saying 'I slept with all my boyfriends, as everyone did'. Nonetheless, by no means all the Sixty Somethings were what might be termed sexually liberated. 'Sex? No, I was too busy being good,' said Molly, who represented a certain proportion of the sample as a whole.

Although there was a view, as Betty suggested, that the Pill meant that women of her age had the sex that their parents probably hadn't, there was also acknowledgement that sexual permissiveness has always gone in waves and that they weren't the first to be promiscuous or have sex outside marriage. Indeed, Pat Thane's 2014 discourse *Happy Families?: Realities of Family Life in Twentieth Century Britain* pointed out how illegitimacy rates were particularly high in the 1860s. However, what was different for the Sixty Somethings was that the Pill meant that sex came without the risk of pregnancy. It may have ushered in greater sexual permissiveness, but it was also a response to need. The war had encouraged sexual liberation. The uncertainties of the time, and the risks faced by young men sent to fight, led young people to feel that if they didn't make love, or get married, when they could, they might not get another chance. From a deeply puritanical family, Katie's mother admitted in her eighties that she had slept with Katie's father once before they were married. 'He was going to war. We thought we might never see each other again.' The Sixties were in this way, as in many others, immensely affected by the war and what had gone before.

Thus the Pill was seen as a catalyst and, according to Frances, the change in sexual politics and sexual relations was 'immense'. As Annie expressed it, her generation felt they were much more open-minded than their parents, even though few seemed to have discussed the matter with their families. Many got their contraception secretly and Verity told how her mother was 'absolutely beside herself with horror to find out I was on the Pill'. Melissa got pregnant at 18: she didn't tell her mother but sorted out her own termination, as 'there was no way I was going to discuss it with my family. They never knew. I wouldn't have done that to them.'

Certainly not everyone found themselves easily drawn into this new sexual landscape, particularly when sexual liberation was in strong opposition to the values they had grown up with. Barbara provides a good example. Describing herself as a very prudish teenager, she was brought up as a Catholic and had it 'rammed down her throat' that she had to be a virgin when she married. It took her a long time to come to the view that it was all right if she was not. Despite considering herself on the liberal side, and although she had sexual relationships before marriage, her feelings were always in conflict. Poppy too experienced anxiety and personal dilemma about sex outside marriage. Also from a Catholic background, she grew up believing it was absolutely unacceptable and a mortal sin. At the same time she espoused feminism and felt she 'needed to be out there having sex', being equal with men. Her personal dilemma led to a lot of anxiety and guilt. She began by justifying sex in the belief that it would lead to marriage, but then had to have a rethink as the 'it's okay if I'm going to marry them' didn't fit with her lifestyle. 'I then had to free up and think, just go for it.' Julia, who said she was 'quite a permissive girl' and 'had a great time really', still admitted to being somewhat confused and neurotic about sex. Alice too said she was always very conflicted about sex, which didn't mean it didn't happen, but she always felt terribly guilty about it. A number of women also mentioned how the fear of pregnancy still hung over them even though they were taking the Pill. The impression from the women was that sex wasn't quite the simple hedonistic pleasure it was often made out to be.

Moreover, there was another less positive side to this picture of new-found sexual freedom. Phrases such as 'a double-edged sword' were repeated time after time as so many of women, looking back at their experiences, told of the pressures they'd faced to have sex they might have preferred to go without. Often they thought they would behave differently if they had their chance again. Lissa recalled 'a few years in which I didn't have very good relationships and far too many of them' and Hazel Grace said, 'I went out with all these alpha males and womanisers and they were all uniformly terrible lovers.' She added that you 'don't really discover your sexuality until you're with someone who loves and is devoted to you. Certainly you don't discover it by sleeping with a lot of random arseholes.' Katherine too remembered having lots of sex and one-night stands and losing her virginity at 19 because she felt she was 'lagging behind'. She added, 'I don't remember enjoying much of it at all. You had to.' 'Most people I know look back and wonder what was I doing, what was that all about?' said Jacca.

In retrospect, there was a prevailing view that the Pill had its pros and cons. It liberated women in a sense and, according to Lynne, sexual freedom was part of the reason why she and her friends were not tied into long-term relationships like their parents. Most women saw the changes positively, but there was the view too, voiced by Charlotte, that 'standards and morals came down within my peer group'. The greater sexual freedom could sometimes also apparently licence what was in fact abusive behaviour. Geraldine recalled how 'some guy at a party stuck his tongue down my throat. I was outraged and walked off. When I got back people were laughing at me. Perhaps they'd said I was uptight or a frigid bitch or other terms used at the time.' Winifred too remembered a couple of 'very narrow escapes sexually' in London. She iterated how there had been a tendency for men to think that 'because this sexual permissiveness thing was starting up' anyone was fair game. 'And you had to fight against that.' Jude spoke of her time as an unattached young woman in London. Men she met at parties would assume she would go to bed with them and she felt obliged to comply. 'It meant I had a lot of bad sex.'

Maureen concluded that free love was not all it was cracked up to be, and Jenny said that although it felt like liberation, women were never actually 'on a par with blokes'. In her view, women were able to sleep with as many people as they chose to, but they were still looking for love, while men were looking for sex. As Zena pointed out, the Pill had made matters worse by making it more difficult for the girl to say no.

Drugs

Reflections on the sixties and seventies almost certainly conjure up a picture that includes the rising visibility and use of recreational drugs, particularly among young people. The Wootton Report of 1968 estimated that up to a third of a million people in Britain had tried cannabis and that convictions for possession of the drug in Britain doubled between 1965 and 1966 and then doubled again in the following year. By this latter date, three-quarters of those arrested for a drug offence were white and under 25 years. The use of recreational drugs was on course to increase yet further. Leo Benedictus, writing in the *Guardian* in February 2011, states, 'It is estimated that the number of young adults in Britain who had tried an illegal drug in the 1960s was fewer than 5%. This reached roughly 10% in the 1970s, and 15–20% in the 1980s. By 1995, nearly half of all young people said they had taken drugs.'

Illegal drugs were widely publicised at the time as characterising the prevailing 'sex, drugs and rock 'n' roll' youth culture. Epitomised by Scott McKenzie's song 'San Francisco (Be Sure to Wear Flowers in Your Hair)' the 1967 'Summer of Love' became the first high-profile event of this new counterculture. Attended by some half a million people, it was all about protest, against conformity, against materialism, against the Vietnam War. Students in their thousands apparently left their studies for a summer of sex, drugs and rock 'n' roll. The drug culture was also highly visible at the Woodstock Festival in upstate New York in 1969, attended by almost half a million people and billed as 'three days of peace and music', just as it was at the Isle of Wight festivals of 1968, 1969 and, notably, 1970. So prevalent were drugs at this last festival that the police offered a drugs amnesty, albeit with no takers.

For many, drug-taking was mingled with a fascination for various forms of mysticism. Psychedelic music, incense burning and Eastern dress were among the visible signs of this nod towards a wider culture. The Beatles also travelled to the ashram of the guru Maharishi Mahesh Yogi in India, while others dabbled with the Mexican shamanism explored in the books of Carlos Castaneda. These influences unsurprisingly spilled over into the lyrics and melodies of some music of the time. 'Lucy in the

Sky with Diamonds', for example, is a song credited to John Lennon and Paul McCartney that appears on the Beatles' 1967 *Sgt. Pepper's Lonely Hearts Club Band* album. There has long been speculation, denied by both John and Paul, that the title of this track deliberately stands for the initialism LSD.

There was a very mixed picture of participation in a drug culture among the Sixty Somethings. Not all gave direct information on this point but, of those who did, 15 categorically stated they had never taken drugs, six implied drugs had been part of normal life, four suggested they had taken them for a while and twelve said they had tried substances but not in any very serious way.

Many of those who had not tried recreational drugs said they had never been offered any, they were 'too conservative and scared of the world' to take them, or they just weren't part of a sex, drugs and rock 'n' roll generation. Zena commented that although lots of weed was passed round at university, she didn't join in because she couldn't stand the fog caused by smoking. Theresa described herself as 'a hippy without the drugs'.

On the other hand, some women said they had used recreational drugs over the years, and smoked quite a bit of dope when younger. Jo said this was common in the broadcasting world, where they made lots of excuses, such as that it made you more creative. Several of the women in this group intimated that they gave drugs up over time when they became bored with them, or felt taking them conflicted with their responsibilities as parents.

Lesser users suggested that because drugs were around, they'd have a go. Most, however, said they didn't do much for them or, as suggested by Frances, 'life seemed colourful enough' without them. These women had rarely tried anything other than the 'odd puff of marijuana'.

Rock 'n' roll

As suggested, music had a central place in the lives of many young people during the sixties and seventies. It was 'very special', said Annie, and 'hugely important', according to Barbara. According to Theresa, 'I couldn't have lived without the music. The music was the generation.' 'The Beatles came along, then the Stones. Oh my God!' added Katherine. For Poppy, rock 'n' roll music was 'a big part of everything'. She was always playing music and going to gigs.

Quite apart from the highly publicised festivals, such as Woodstock and the Isle of Wight, there was a growth in pop concerts across the country, in local theatres, halls and on university campuses, as well as a proliferation of live music in pubs and other venues across the land. This was a lifeline for many young people at the time. Talking about the sixties, Zena told how she 'went to school, came home, did homework, watched limited programmes on TV ... so friends and I went to concerts ... that was our hobby, shall I say.' Deirdre also recalled going to pop concerts packed with screaming girls. 'I wasn't really moved to scream myself, but I did my best to join in to see what it felt like,' she said.

Music was also much more accessible to young audiences than in the past. Most towns had at least one record shop where you could go after school and at weekends to listen to selected 45 rpm 7" 'singles' in special little booths that would just fit two. Programmes aimed at a young audience also proliferated. 'Pop' music had first appeared on British television on *Juke Box Jury* with David Jacobs on Saturday evenings, which ran for eight years from 1959. Well-spoken and conventionally dressed, Jacobs was challenged from 1961 by ITV's more 'with it' *Thank Your Lucky Stars* (1961–1966) and *Ready Steady Go!* (1963–1966). The

BBC replied with *Top of the Pops*, which became their flagship music show from 1964 to 2006. This featured live bands and a live audience and attracted some 15 million viewers a week.

'Trannies' too became ubiquitous among young people, who could listen to them wherever they went and even continue under the sheets when they went to bed. According to Retrowow, over two million transistor radios were sold to people in Britain in 1961, and sales continued to grow over the next decades. There were many things to listen to, from weekly programmes such as BBC Radio's *Pick of the Pops* with Alan Freeman, which had a regular Sunday afternoon slot from 1962 to 1972, to radio stations with differing provenance. Early competition came from Radio Luxembourg, a commercial popular music station reaching the British Isles through powerful transmitters. Their English-language service had been running since 1933 but became very popular in Britain in the 1960s. Then the 'pirate radio' stations began arriving, led by Radio Caroline in 1964. It was run originally from a boat moored off Felixstowe to counter broadcasting regulations and the BBC's monopoly and quickly gained a cult following. To counter this challenge, the BBC introduced Radio 1, first broadcast in 1967, the establishment's station offering all-hours pop music.

There were also publications devoted to popular artists and new forms of music that came out weekly and were enthusiastically received by an avid fan base. The *New Musical Express*, established in 1952, became widely read in the 1960s, reaching its peak audience of over 300,000 in 1964. Its main focus was pop music during the 1960s and was a major source of information on pop charts, contemporary groups and artists, and concerts. Deirdre remembered getting this weekly and reading every single word before passing it on to her brother. The *Melody Maker* was another well-known and longer-established music newspaper at the time. This publication had a broader musical focus and had overtaken the *New Musical Express* in the popularity stakes by the early 1970s.

It is groups such as the Beatles and the Rolling Stones that are perhaps best remembered from the 1960s, but the explosion of new artists and forms of music at the time went way beyond the pop scene. Before rock 'n' roll reached Britain, in the mid-1950s, the young had listened to jazz, either 'trad' or the modern jazz favoured by 'beatniks'. Some became involved in the folk music revival of the 1950s, while others favoured imported American blues music or home-grown versions of skiffle. Throughout the 1960s, there was also a heightened visibility of other genres, such as country and western and soul, often crossing the Atlantic from America.

The Sixty Somethings highlighted how the music of their youth was not simply entertainment, it represented their culture and lifestyle. Fans of *Ready Steady Go!* were not only appreciating the music but also idolising its host. Poppy and Verity both said they had curly hair but that they, and lots of their friends, wanted to look like Cathy McGowan. They both used to iron their hair although, according to Poppy, it still frizzed in the rain.

The music of the 1960s and 1970s, moreover, felt different and special. This was exemplified by the high profile of events such as Woodstock and the Isle of Wight or the Summer of Love, when music was meant to be a large part of what they were all about even if the publicity often seemed to have a different focus. 'The music had something to say,' said Jacca, and 'it underscored drugs and psychedelic drugs,' added Verity. Moreover, and very importantly, it was 'linked into politics' for Lynne and 'to protest, optimism and real issues … and not just love' for Annie. The women recalled artists such as Joan Baez and Bob Dylan who had sung about rebellion and revolution and how music had become a medium for the protest taking place in other forms and settings. Winifred said that 'if I could pinpoint one thing that changed while I was young, it would be that we went from just tunes and music to really essential poetic lyrics that meant something'. Sylvie also talked about how a growing interest in blues was not only about the music itself but also about opening people up to another culture in America.

Another predominant recollection was that the music of the time belonged to young people. Rather than being miniature adults, and sharing music with older generations, they had something that was their own. There was a feeling among the women that this was something new. And they liked it, especially the way it could provoke parental disapproval. 'It was part of the enjoyment,' said Violet. Many mentioned how their music shocked and horrified their parents and drew a wedge between them. Elvis Presley (nicknamed 'Elvis the Pelvis' for his suggestive gyrations) and the Rolling Stones were particularly singled out for parental disapproval. Katherine agreed with Eleanor, who said 'Elvis was blamed for corrupting a generation with his naughty hip movements.' 'Are you going to turn that ghastly noise down?' Dolly's uncle had asked when Mick Jagger was playing, 'I'm sure he takes the horns off his head every morning.'

Music therefore provided an identity distinct from that of their parents. The women described how people aligned themselves with each other through music. Sometimes these countercultural and subcultural identities crossed class boundaries and sometimes they didn't. Long-haired 'hippies' and alternative 'freaks' were often middle class, warring 'mods' and 'rockers' were more likely to be working class.

The appetite for music also coincided with hormonal development and arrived in the context of a changing view of the world, as discussed later in this chapter. It was associated with creativity and freedom of expression, and it expressed a prevailing ethos of the day that was anti-war and in favour of nuclear disarmament. As Jenny said, 'Music gave identity to an emerging group of people who wanted to look at the world differently.' Nonetheless, music reflected a diversity of tastes and spoke to people at different levels.

The identity conferred by music was further reflected in the way young people dressed at the time. Essential markers of cultural identity, fashions could come and go at dizzying speed. The beatniks' black polo-neck sweaters and drainpipe trousers gave way to miniskirts, Chelsea boots and then psychedelic shirts and blouses, only to be junked in favour of platform heels, maxi skirts, kaftans and Afghan coats. Blue jeans, especially Levi's, have survived in various cuts to this day, while flares, bell-bottoms, ultra-wide 'loon' pants (sometimes with inserted darts in contrasting patterns) and 'Oxford bags' came and went.

Lindyloo pointed out how clothing and fashion went with your music. Fans of the Beatles might not be fans of the Rolling Stones, and those appreciating Dylan might not also appreciate The Seekers. Pop artists of the day conveyed their own personal image which could be reflected in the self-portrayal of their followers.

Music hadn't touched all the women to the same degree. A few said they weren't very musical themselves or that while they had listened to pop music in their young days, it had never been particularly important to them. Some had been more interested in literature or the theatre, and these other art forms had been just as significant in reflecting the cultural changes going on at the time. Winifred, for example, mentioned the influence of iconic drama such as the plays of Samuel Beckett or the musical *Hair*, and Lilian cited the important influence of the radical psychiatrist R.D. Laing. Most women, nonetheless, felt that music of the day had left an important legacy. Children of the Sixty Somethings still listened to sixties music, and large music festivals had become a permanent fixture. Barbara and Lissa were among those who hadn't realised the uniqueness of sixties music at the time, and Sarah felt it has survived because it was good. The women themselves still enjoy the same music partly because, as Alison said, 'modern music doesn't have the memories that go with it.'

Typical hippies?

The term 'hippy' came from America in the mid-sixties and originally referred to a counterculture of beatniks living in Greenwich Village, New York, and in the Haight-Ashbury quarter of San Francisco. Although the term gained widespread popularity around the world, an image of a hippy is easier to conjure up than to describe. According to the *Oxford English Dictionary*, a hippy is '(Especially in the 1960s) a person of unconventional appearance, typically having long hair, associated with a subculture involving a rejection of conventional values and the taking of hallucinogenic drugs.' The UK Hippy website states: 'We know too well that the word hippy evokes different feelings in different people. For some it conjures up memories of love and peace, the swinging sixties and bell-bottom trousers, while for others it takes us back to the days of Stonehenge Free Festival and the Peace Convoy. From protest marches to altered states of consciousness, from alternative spirituality to free love and from campervans to communes, that one word captures it all.' So how hippy or countercultural were the Sixty Somethings back in the day?

Probably the majority were influenced in some way or other by the events and ethos of the time even if they didn't think of themselves as hippies or participate in a counterculture in any direct way. It was more that they were a part of a strong youth culture with its own attitudes and mores. Lilian summed up her experience: 'The influence of a hippy era was pretty strong. I was not one of the cool kids, rather old-fashioned to say the least, but nonetheless I was affected by that sort of thing ... All the peace and love stuff of the hippy era. People can make fun of it, but I think it has huge value actually. It enabled people to think differently, and unconventionally, about how they wanted to live. The values they had were hugely positive.'

For many, being 'with it' was about being absorbed within the prevailing youth culture. Several achieved this by knowing, or being in contact with, celebrities. Beth, for example, knew Mary Quant, while Sylvie knew Cynthia Lennon and lived near

Paul McCartney and others. As fifteen-year-olds, Katie and two school friends were taken to meet the Beatles at the studio where they were filming *A Hard Day's Night*. Zena had got the Beatles' autographs, and Jemima had sewn up the Kinks' trousers. She had been a friend of the secretary of entertainments at university, where she met the stars and was called upon to undertake the repair. Lissa had worked in fashion in trendy places like Carnaby Street and the Kings Road and did some part-time modelling. She had, in her early twenties, a boyfriend who ran a model agency. He would send her to fashion shoots if the booked model didn't turn up.

Hayley's claim to fame, totally accidentally, was being personally responsible for the song 'Grandad' getting to the top of the charts. She was working in the credit control department of a company where someone wanted 100 copies of the record for family and friends. She recommended they go to HMV in Oxford Street, which just happened to be the shop that the top 10 ratings were based on. For Jenny being part of the scene was knowing many of the young intellectual lefties of the time.

Others liked to feel the atmosphere by living in Biba at lunchtime, or getting the right look. Zena told an amusing story about her mother wanting her to get her hair cut. She was 14 and wouldn't go to her hairdresser but was watching *Ready Steady Go!* on a Friday evening when Vidal Sassoon was on with Cathy McGowan. 'I said I'll go to the hairdressers if I can go to him,' she told her mother, who agreed. So she walked to the phone box at the end of the road, looked up the number in the directory and made an appointment for a Saturday morning. Come the day, she put on what she thought were her best clothes and set out for Bond Street with a friend. A local haircut cost 3/6, but her mother said it would be expensive and had given her £2 plus another £2 for something else she'd asked her to buy. It was an 'out of world experience', with her hair cut by a junior who looked like Roger Daltrey from The Who, but the moment of truth came when it came to pay. She was asked for £4. She had just enough but nothing for a tip, and her mother went berserk because £4 was a weekly wage. Nonetheless, she had her 15 minutes of fame at school on the Monday. Moreover, a friend recently said she'd never forget when she walked into school with a Vidal Sassoon haircut. 'That was popular culture,' said Zena.

Some made other types of gesture towards what might be seen as hippydom. Alison, for example, got as far as buying a bell to wear round her neck, while Hayley called herself a weekend hippy. For her that meant going to Etam and buying a kaftan. Primrose wore a sewn-up blanket in her youth as a protest, Maggie joined a cooperative to set up a wholefood shop and Theresa wore loons, bell-bottom jeans, lots of beads and Jesus sandals: 'I was a folkie rather than a druggy.' With the concurrent influence of the feminist movement, five women (including Mary, who didn't see herself as a hippy) went bra-less for a considerable length of time. There was, however, a price to pay for Beth, who said she ached for days after going on a long march. Bella lived in communes as a student in London, and both Beth and Primrose mentioned spells in squats. Others, such as Sylvie, had lots of middle-class friends on communes or in squats, although they hadn't tried this way of life themselves. Beth nonetheless questioned how revolutionary communal living was. In her experience, women were still doing the housework and cooking in these places. Zena too wondered about the 'whole hippy commune thing', concluding, after spending a month on a kibbutz to see what it was like, that the idealistic view was exaggerated.

Several of the Sixty Somethings had, or would have liked to have, camper vans in their later years. Besides anything else, they were reminiscent of hippy trails in the sixties and seventies. Jenny was the only one to mention such holidays, recalling two trips to Morocco in a green VW van that she thought cost £70. One of her memories was watching the back wheel roll past as nine of them were driving down the Atlas Mountains. Another was the surprise of one of the blokes sleeping outside with his baseball boots under his head as a pillow when he awoke in the morning to find they had gone and been replaced by a basket of figs. Loads of dope was smoked on these trips and 'we nearly went off our rockers'.

If the hippy counterculture tended to be middle class, Maureen was the only one of the Sixty Somethings to mention any involvement with the more significant working-class subcultures like Mods and Rockers, even if she did regard herself as somewhat peripheral. Living in Brighton, she had a Mod boyfriend and, to her mother's horror, rode on the back of his scooter. 'It was all very exciting. Except when it got a bit scary and we ran home ... It got quite nasty.' Usually they went to a nightclub a bit like the Cavern but in Brighton, lying to their parents and saying they were all getting together to work on their A levels. 'Very naughty ... wonderful ... we danced and danced and probably kissed a few boys and had a thoroughly good time.'

Many of the sample had some experience of counter-culturalism through being in the right place at the right time, whether or not they participated strongly in the ongoing activities. Bella went to San Francisco for a year after finishing at art college and recalled having the beads and the bangles, even though the 'flowers in the hair' phase had ended. Chenhalls also went to California, during the Summer of Love, but again didn't remember wearing flowers in her hair. She also went to Australia for three months in 1967 and did recall walking barefoot in Sydney thinking 'this is the life'. 'That was probably about as anti-cultural as I got,' she said.

Deirdre was in Paris as an au pair during the strike and student protests of May 1968, sometimes referred to as *la grève* or *les évènements*, that were brutally suppressed by riot police. Although she was a bystander, she did awake one morning to find the baby she was looking after crying and the parents nowhere to be seen. There was no telephone in the flat, and it was her day off but fortunately she was there to look after the child. In the evening somebody came to tell her that the parents were in prison. Apparently they had been bundled into a police van for being on the streets and watching the fires burn. They returned home the next day. Stephanie had lived in Vancouver for a short time in the seventies. She said it was like a mini San Francisco, with Buddhism, macrobiotic cooking and other ways of thinking that have endured through mindfulness and to which she still subscribes. She's just an old hippy, she says.

The mood of the generation

As the Sixty Somethings were all too aware, it is significant that they were the first generation to be born after the war. Almost without exception, the women emphasised the impact this had had on them. Most, as Olive said, had benefited from what those before them had fought for.

The benefits took a variety of forms. Molly was among those encouraged by her parents to make the most of new opportunities they hadn't had, and to be more socially mobile. This was facilitated by the welfare reforms taking place in the post-war period that included improvements in educational standards and an expansion of higher education. There was also political movement and an aura of change. Mary said this meant that ideas about living conditions, politics, sex and a host of other matters were thrown up in the air. The war shook everyone up to a degree, added Bella. Radical change was afoot.

Much of this radicalism was expressed in high ideals for the future. Young people were not prepared to put up with 'stuff', said Winifred, they wanted to change what they thought was wrong. There was a feeling of release after the war and an opportunity to make things better. The generation was idealistic and peace was going to rule the planet, said Norah. 'I politicised everything,' said Beth, and 'I got up my parents' nose by saying that even food was political.' 'What we did was to rebel,' said Verity, against 'post-war food, post-war dullness' and any other viable target. 'We were going to change the world. The older generation was not seeing what we could see.' Encouragement came in the form of liberal reforms, such as the abolition of capital punishment and greater access to abortion in the 1960s, said Barbara. Things were on track.

With this idealism came a strong sense of personal entitlement, suggested Geraldine. According to Audrey, there was a feeling of total freedom within the generation to do whatever they wanted. She couldn't have had the life she did had she been born before the war. It was the first generation to say that 'well, you might have rules but we're going to break them', said Molly. There was a degree of shouting from the rooftops, according to Tabitha, as it was the first time 'anybody wanted to hear our views'. There was more questioning because there was more education, suggested Persia.

Women such as the Sixty Somethings wanted opportunities. They didn't expect things to be given to them on a plate, but they expected to be able to choose their own directions and take the initiative. Jacca recalls how she would go to a cafe and eat tomato ketchup and sugar lumps because they were free. She didn't think anyone should give her food, but would have been furious had she been stopped from having the ketchup and sugar. She thought members of her generation would have been outraged if they were not allowed to seize opportunities that presented themselves.

Self-confidence and self-esteem came with the territory. 'I felt nobody was better than me,' said Lynne. Jo's father had instilled in her that she could do anything she wanted, and Lilian had been brought up to believe she was no better and no worse than anybody else. They weren't going to be pushed around, said Katherine. And they were happy to question authority, to ask questions. 'In some ways we felt if you don't like something, speak up,' said Margaret. 'From then on, nobody has told me what to do,' added Mary. It was, moreover, a fun time, with not a care in the world, said Jan, and important to live for pleasure, added Alice. There was 'a bit of that pie in the sky optimism in the sixties', according to Lois. 'I think we were on a bit of a high.' It gave freedom to experiment and, said Clara, 'we were going to do the sex, drugs and the rock 'n' roll.' There was a sense of anti-conformity which Flavia suggested 'came from our upbringing because our parents were so authoritarian and their parents were even more so'. She thought there was an air of rebellion in the air, fuelled by the sheer numbers in their generation and the ability to kick against things together.

Jacca wondered if this 'mood' had emerged through a rather small window. Was it something to do with a very specific time? She had been in her early teens when the Beatles had 'happened'. If she'd been eighteen, or five, she wouldn't have given them a second thought. She was in the right space. She saw them as the working class sticking two fingers up at the establishment, religion and everything else. 'I was just old enough to get it but not too old to be beyond it.' When she was 15, 16 and 17, just as she was becoming a young adult, it was Bob Dylan and protest songs that came and at 17, 18, 19 and 20 it was the Happy Hippy stuff: lots of dope, flower power, free love and everything else. 'Again I was exactly the right age to be enjoying that.' She thought the timing had been critical for her and that someone born in, say, 1964 would have had a completely different experience.

Despite all outward signs of liberation, and a disrespect for gratuitous rules and restrictions, some women did question how anti-authoritarian and unconventional they really had been. Although they were distinct from their parents, the generations were not always too dissimilar from one another. As Lois expressed it, 'My sense was that people were very much following, whether it was about fashion, or the way people conducted their lives, there were ways of doing things. Maybe a bit freer than before, but still expectations remained.'

Indeed, Betty suggested everyone at university conformed in their resistance to conformity. Alice agreed that new norms on sex, drugs and rock 'n' roll, for instance, had taken over. Zena talked about a phase in the early sixties in the East End when the preferred attire was a dolly rocker dress, covered by a blue Bri-Nylon mac and brown suede laced Hush Puppies. This identikit fashion was seen by the older generation as totally non-conformist. However, 'the fact that everybody of a certain age was wearing these things seemed to pass them by.' Margaret made a similar point. She said it was actually quite hard to be an individualist and, in fashion, you had to fit into one tribe or another. She recounted how she'd decided to wear a midi skirt when 'you had to wear a miniskirt', describing the looks and comments she got and saying 'that was the worst day of my life'. It was fine to try things to shock parents, but 'woe betide you' if you stepped outside what your friends thought was okay.

Overall there was more conforming to unconventional things than anti-conformity as such. This had struck Deirdre, who had visited a school with a reputation for freedom and liberal values. Although there was no school uniform as such, all pupils seemed to subscribe to a dress code of jeans and t-shirts. Presumably anyone showing any sign of deviation would have felt extremely uncomfortable. Patricia probably spoke for many when she said her generation was much more conformist than it would have liked to admit at the time.

A culture of their own

It was towards the end of the war that the term 'teenager' was first used in America. Jon Savage charted its origins in his 2007 book *Teenage: The Creation of Youth 1875–1945*, an authoritative historical account of how the concept of the teenager came about. He suggested, contrary to much conventional wisdom, that youth culture did not develop from scratch in the 1950s. In particular he cited the influence of the psychologist G. Stanley Hall who, controversially at the beginning of the twentieth century, introduced the idea of adolescence as a time of storm and stress. Others before him had also described a transitional period between puberty and adulthood, even if it had not been given a specific name.

The Sixty Somethings may not have been the first generation identified as 'youth', but there is little doubt they pursued a lifestyle different to anything that had gone before. It was the Swinging Sixties, and the cities were discarding the drabness of the war years and becoming exciting places to be. Things were happening, too, which had never been believed possible. In 1969, for instance, men landed on the moon. It was a 'seminal' time when young people broke away from the strictures and prejudices of their parents, said Helen; they were not just mini adults. It was a golden age, suggested Frances: 'we were freed from older patterns of thought.' Partly as a reaction to the ending of the war, many young people saw themselves as anti-authoritarian and unconventional thinkers who were willing to speak up for themselves and have their own views.

It was not just thought, however, that began to divide the generations. Many of the women stressed how they were the first generation to have a culture distinct from that of their parents. Music, as the women have already described, was a key part of this. The Beatles and the 'Mersey Sound', the Rolling Stones and the countless pop stars that became household names, Bob Dylan and others singing about protest, the import of blues and rock and soul from America, and much more – there was endless choice. The cinema was also important. Everyone will have had their favourite films but *Bonnie and Clyde*, *Easy Rider*, *Midnight Cowboy*, *Woodstock* and *Alice's Restaurant* stand out among the iconic. Television dramas, such as *Up the Junction* and *Cathy Come Home*, also made their mark on the more politicised within the generation.

Moreover, there was not a single culture but a wide variety of counter- and subcultures on offer. Jukeboxes had appeared in the UK shortly after the war and rapidly became a feature of the new milk bars and coffee bars. The opening of the first Wimpy Bar, Britain's first chain of burger bars, in 1954, was another symbolic event, helping to export the developing American youth culture to this country, soon followed by other imports from America that Deirdre remembered as 'fish fingers, hula hoops and flip-flops'. As television became more widespread, American culture became increasingly familiar through a rich array of programmes, from *I Love Lucy* to *The Phil Silvers Show*, with Silvers as the rascally Sergeant Bilko, and *Dragnet*, the first US-imported cop show. Later, the Beatles were among those introducing mysticism and spirituality to anyone interested. Young people could variously identify as mods, rockers, hippies or anything else they chose, even if choices were often class-related, confirming their allegiance through what they wore and ate, their music, how they lived and what they believed in.

Clothes were very important during these years, probably because the old conventions were being thrown out. Young people didn't want to wear the same as their mothers any more. Mary Quant and others led the fashion trail, with models as distinct as Twiggy and Jean Shrimpton becoming icons of the age. Brightly coloured clothes, paper dresses, bell-bottoms, miniskirts, beaded kaftans and many other varieties of attire prevailed. Jeans entered centre stage, where they've remained ever since. Many, but not all of the women seemed to have enjoyed shocking parents. Meg said they had revelled in wearing miniskirts and being scruffy. And wearing platform shoes in the seventies was all about showing off. 'You wouldn't do it to enjoy yourself,' she said. 'I think our parents were horrified but I thought it was wonderful,' said Maureen.

The expansion of higher education played an important role in developing and promoting youth culture. It was a key context in which young people shared ideas and protested against what they didn't like. Liza talked about the 'me, me, me' generation, and several others agreed that there was time to form your own opinions rather than have them thrust upon you. 'As adolescents we did a lot of thinking about things,' said Annie, and 'once you've started thinking for yourself, it's very empowering,' added Winifred. Others concurred. Jacca talked about the way she and her contemporaries had bonded through their shared interests and ideals. They'd read the same books and listened to the same music, and there was a common sense of identity. There was, too, 'something about sitting around getting stoned talking about almost nothing' she said.

The notion of a 'me' generation was, however, tempered by an accompanying concern for society at large, suggested Geraldine. The women talked about a growing humanitarianism, environmentalism and awareness of other sentient creatures with rights. The strong anti-war sentiment led to a shift towards thinking globally about other communities and human beings, suggested Flavia. Notions of class, race and gender also began to shift, said Primrose. The focus was on meaningfulness rather than capitalism, suggested Poppy, and for some it became fashionable to be working class and frugal. As Jacca said, 'we wanted to keep down with the Joneses.' Jo added how being working class and from the North gave you status, while Maggie regretted not joining a drama society at the time: 'But it was all middle class and I wasn't going to do anything middle class.'

At the same time the church was losing its hold for many, perhaps because of war and people questioning things, said Bella. 'Where was God,' then? Moreover, the church was seen by many as out-of-date and no longer necessary for respectability. As people became increasingly in control of their own lives, they became less reliant on the church for their identity, said Lois.

A time to protest

Another defining characteristic of the developing youth culture, with its confidence and ideals, was that young people were not afraid to challenge authority and voice their concerns. It was an age of protest. At university many women became involved in the numerous splintering, and often warring, Marxist groups, a phenomenon satirised by the various Judean resistance factions in *Monty Python's Life of Brian*.

There was, however, a continuum of involvement and motivation. Some Sixty Somethings had been very actively involved in campaigning and protest and these, according to Katherine, formed a very vocal minority. Barbara, for instance, had been going on demonstrations from the age of 13, and Jo said she should be lumped in with the left-wing protestors. Lilian's life had been 'absolutely bound up' in the labour and trade union movement and all that that implied, and Ruby identified herself with the protest part of her generation. Membership of higher education institutions or trade unions often provided a setting and impetus for action.

Other women joined demonstrations on a more occasional basis. They might have had a particular issue of concern, or they might just have gone along with what everyone else was doing. It was impossible to avoid getting involved in the 1968 protests at university, said Helen. And Lois joined sit-ins when she first got to university 'because it seemed like fun'. She only later realised what they were all about. Sylvie too took part in demonstrations but didn't always know what they were for. Generally there was a lot of publicity for strikes and marches and people came along to join in. According to Hayley, some people liked a good demonstration, especially as it didn't bring the risks of retribution that had been the case in the past.

The protest movement bypassed a considerable number of Sixty Somethings. Jemima hated protesting and Deirdre disliked the way student politics went overboard on an issue one week only for it to be completely forgotten the next. Others weren't particularly political, weren't in the right place at the right time or thought it was not something they should be doing. There wasn't a strong ethos of protest when Alison got to university and her fellow students were quite apathetic and uninterested in political issues. Nonetheless, there were organised coach trips to protests in London which some of them would go on. Once they got to London, however, they would spend the day shopping in Oxford Street, returning to the coach in time for the journey home.

Several key issues were particularly likely to outrage the women. Anti-nuclear protest was a 'huge thing', said Audrey, and her comment was endorsed by others. In August 1945, towards the end of the war, American B-29 bombers had dropped atomic bombs on the Japanese cities of Hiroshima and Nagasaki, immediately killing an estimated 120,000 people and leaving many more with radiation poisoning. In 1952, the US tested the first thermonuclear weapon, the 'H-Bomb', vastly more powerful and destructive than the bombs dropped on Japan, and nuclear proliferation was well under way. By the end of the 1950s there had been more than 300 nuclear tests. The Campaign for Nuclear Disarmament, with a large female membership, was formed in 1957, as a first step in the anti-war movement.

Although mostly too young to have joined CND at its outset, the campaign and its messages had a direct legacy for the Sixty Somethings. Many talked about living in the shadow of the bomb. Several said they'd been terrified about being 'nuked' into oblivion and, as Maggie said, 'we were all waiting for the revolution to come, so none of this mattered really.' Why worry about tomorrow? Hazel Grace recalled how her mother had taken her to school on 'the day the world was supposed to end' during the Cuban Missile Crisis of October 1962. She had wanted to spend a last perfect day with her. It had all had a great impact on her. She had been worried all the time, particularly when she'd been pregnant and had a small baby. Living near to GCHQ and feeling a likely target, she'd kept the curtains closed and got the cellar ready.

The 1968 Grosvenor Square protest against the Vietnam War had been attended by a number of the women. This was the first big march Jenny had been to and she'd been terrified by the horses charging into the crowd. Having lost a shoe, she remembered running down the road with only one on. She was still at college at the time, but had gone to this march with a woman she'd met on a train. It wasn't until she went to London and met lots of 'lefties' that she really got politically involved.

Other concerns were also apparent. Jo said her marching and shouting had always been about the environment, workers' rights, pay and politics, and never about feminism or gay liberation. Lilian had been involved with a range of issues, including gay rights issues, which she strongly believed in. Ruby had campaigned for lots of platforms over her lifetime and was part of the Jewish Socialist Group concerned with opposing Zionism.

Some Sixty Somethings, with hindsight, regretted not taking a more active part in the protest movement. 'I missed out on a whole experience there,' said Tweegy, while Frances condemned herself for not protesting enough. It had been fashionable to be protesting, said Geraldine, but there had also been genuine energy behind it. It was all part of rejecting capitalism and being anti-authority, explained Poppy. 'Our generation didn't want to just accept the rules that were passed down.' And it was also about respecting life and people and not just economics. The reaction against war was also an important part of it.

Men and women

The sixties and seventies saw an ever-increasing awareness and intolerance of inequalities between the sexes. The introduction of the contraceptive pill in 1961, and its availability to all regardless of marital status in 1974, was a landmark step in giving women greater control over their fertility, but there was much else yet to be changed. The feminist movement, or women's liberation as it was popularly called (often shortened to 'Women's Lib'), was gaining ground, with support and pressure groups springing up around the country. Strikes for equal pay – notably the Ford machinists' strike in Dagenham in 1968 – were also taking place. Campaigning seemed to gain some results, with legislation to give women improved rights in relation to property ownership, sex discrimination, employment and domestic violence introduced over this period.

The Sixty Somethings were very vocal on the subject of men and could point to many disadvantages they had faced as young women. They thought men were given more freedom, better apprenticeships and more chance of getting into Oxford and Cambridge universities. They also said a job was often regarded as a 'holding operation' for a woman until she got married, and that sleeping around was okay for men but not women. 'In a word, it was all still hugely slanted towards the men,' said Barbara. Nearer home, Betty said her aunt and mother-in-law always saw men as the important ones, and Lois said her mother 'definitely subscribed to the view that you gave the men bigger portions of food'.

Women also felt they'd had to 'put up with' men on a daily basis. Barbara told how those of her age would talk about women as objects. 'Oh, I like her but I'm not keen on her legs' or 'She's pretty but her nose is a bit too snub,' they might say in front of the women as if it didn't matter. She said they took it for granted that women could be talked about in that way. Zena agreed that you were identified as a female by your attractiveness to males which, incidentally, she didn't think had changed very much since. Verity added that men had no compunction about putting up pictures of scantily dressed females in public workspaces and nobody said a word. She also recalled record album covers with women in hardly any clothes and said the only time you'd see scantily clad males was when some star wanted to show himself off.

More notice also tended to be taken of men. Poppy said she'd increasingly felt absolutely and utterly outraged, seeing ten times a day how women had less power. She gave the example of going to a meeting and saying something and nobody taking any notice, followed by a man saying exactly the same thing two minutes later and being told it was a good idea and would be noted. She also thought men were seen and served more quickly than women in pubs and bars. Rachel felt men were always at an advantage, whether at home, at university or at work. She too thought their behaviour and views were given precedence and it felt as if one had to compete with them all the time. Alice said you had to try a lot harder and be more assertive if you were a woman. She then recalled a classic exchange with her boss. She'd wanted to go on an assertiveness training course and he'd asked her if she didn't think she was assertive enough. She replied, 'I suppose so,' and didn't go on the course.

Harassment and embarrassment were also recalled. Alison said you expected sexual harassment as a young girl, but you toughened up and gave as good as you got. However, it wasn't always easy, especially where there was an additional power relationship. Barbara said an eminent professor had his hand on her knee throughout lunch when she went for her first job, and Deirdre had been propositioned by somebody else in a similar position. It could be difficult even as a student. Sylvie, for instance, spoke of a run in with a 'Jack the Lad' tutor who'd made a pass at her, and Tweegy described attempts to embarrass female medical students. She told of an occasion during a lecture on hernias in which an elderly man with lots of lumps and bumps was presented as the patient. The lecturer 'chose me [wearing a bright pink sweater] to come down and examine him. And in those days to examine a hernia you knelt on the floor in front of the man stripped from the waist down. And he chose me, a female, and then questioned and questioned and one knew he wanted me to break down and cry and run away.' She said girls were given a tough time and quite regularly questioned until they wept. In some ways she thought it was a good thing because 'medicine is stressful and you've got to be able to cope with stress'. Other tutors, she said, 'were ready whenever there was an opportunity for a quick snog'.

Generally the women coped and there were some advantages, even if minor. Men would usually pay if you went out, and might hold the door open. Several said they might engineer further advantages through the use of feminine wiles, perhaps 'taking extreme care to show just enough leg' in the right circumstances, although whether or not it made any difference, nobody knew. Sometimes the tactic was to join in. Verity remembered the sexist jokes from Rag Week and how the women laughed and thought they were an act of rebellion. One she remembered was: 'I was graped last night.' 'Do you mean you were raped?' 'No, there was a bunch of them.'

On the whole, however, the women's experiences reinforced their commitment to greater equality and, in many cases, the women's cause. The British suffragette movement, led by Emmeline Pankhurst and her daughter Christabel, had been successful in helping to gain the vote for women, enacted through the Representation of the People Act 1918, giving the franchise to property-owning women over 30, and the Representation of the People (Equal Franchise) Act 1928, extending it to everyone over 21. However, the movement had lost momentum during the war and in the immediate post-war period when women were returned to their homes amid a prevailing ethos that children were best looked after by their mothers. Although there is some controversy on the matter, the second wave of feminism is usually dated as beginning in the 1970s. The start of this decade saw the publication of highly influential texts which became obligatory reading for the new feminists. Foremost among these were *Sexual Politics* by Kate Millett in 1970, which outlined the sexism in the writings of D.H. Lawrence, Norman Mailer and Henry Miller, *The Female Eunuch* by Germaine Greer, also in 1970, which looked at women's self-perceptions throughout history, and Erica Jong's *Fear of Flying* in 1973, a novel about female sexuality.

Many of the Sixty Somethings had been involved in discussion and exploration of feminism and women's issues, and Alison had had the interesting experience of Germaine Greer as a guest lecturer for a term. Those born during the post-war baby boom were 'just trying to get equal pay with blokes', said Lynne. The concerns went wider too. Meg, for instance, pointed to the links between feminism and homelessness and the impact of the 1966 television Wednesday Play *Cathy Come Home* that had highlighted the problem. More broadly the women were concerned with the many ways in which they felt their half of the population was disadvantaged.

Reactions to the women's movement were varied, but for some it was mind-changing. Geraldine, for instance, said she had become radicalised into feminism overnight and 'It was massively exhilarating, I cannot tell you.' She developed a sense of sisterhood she hadn't had before and it was 'very intense'. Lissa described her 'light-bulb moment' when attending university during her adult years. Her English literature tutor had introduced them to *The Handmaid's Tale* by Margaret Atwood and *Oranges Are Not the Only Fruit* by Jeanette Winterson, both published in 1985, and it was a 'revelation'. By the end of the term she had realised how much she had been disadvantaged and how men really were in control. It was something she'd never really thought about before. Many others too said they had been strongly into feminism and talked about the bonding between women and the mutual support they provided. They also told of friends who chose lesbian relationships so that they could have sexual relationships that didn't involve men.

Feminism, nonetheless, meant different things to different women. Jenny pointed to a distinction between socialist feminists, liberal feminists and radical feminists. She had been 'scared stiff' of the third group, who were very militant and had stopped her joining a march because she had her small son in tow. She said she 'felt like a pariah because I had a boy'. She considered herself a socialist feminist. 'We were all doing terribly lefty community-type work,' she said. Others too were wary of the radical feminists. Maggie considered herself a feminist but never subscribed to 'bra burning and all men are evil', and Audrey was not comfortable with feminism that excluded men. Verity and Skelton were among those to say that extreme forms of feminism were difficult for men to cope with and left them feeling a bit insecure about their place in the world.

Many women supported the ideals of feminism but stood on the sidelines. Some were put off by the ideological extremes, whereas others had other pressures bearing on them. Carol, for example, saw herself as a feminist but followed a traditional route as she was still influenced by her parents, and Jacca felt a bit guilty she hadn't been more involved as she had still benefited from the results. Barbara supported all the goals of the women's movement but was too busy building her career to be actively involved.

Indeed, for many of the Sixty Somethings, reality was about to kick in as they moved out of adolescence and young adulthood into the main stage of their adult years. This was to be the longest phase of their lives, when the priorities of work and families became paramount. Their accounts of their lives at this time are outlined in the next chapter.

5

The Adult Years

There came a time, sooner or later, when most of the Sixty Somethings turned their attention to issues such as finding a long-term partner, having children, earning a living, establishing a career and buying a house. Not all of them did all these things and, as they would be the first to admit, their paths did not always run smoothly. Nonetheless, the years of their adult maturity formed a long and crucial phase in their lives, during which they may have raised families and achieved a personal identity through their employment. Inevitably, they would have a significant impact on their later years. They were also a time when the women may have felt that their social status became different from that of their parents.

Finding and losing love

The Sixty Somethings may have been sexually liberated by the Pill and the mood of the generation, but the vast majority of them still made a formal commitment to a partner at some point. Overall, 59 said they had been married and eight said they had not. One of the unmarried had had a civil partnership with another woman. In addition, fourteen of the married group had been married more than once, with one woman having married three times, and almost half reporting more than one live-in relationship over the course of their lives. Twenty-eight of the 67 had experienced divorce and six had been widowed. Most women had cohabited in some way during their lives. In contrast to their parents, the Sixty Somethings had greater experience of multiple cohabitations and marriages, as well as divorce.

Office for National Statistics figures and other official statistics confirm these patterns within the population as a whole, showing that most women married at least once between the end of the war and the early 1970s, when rates began to decline. The falling popularity of marriage was accompanied by an increase in divorce. This gained impetus from the Divorce Reform Act 1969, which came into force at the beginning of 1971 and made the legal process much easier. Also important at this time was the rise in female employment and hence women's greater economic independence.

Cohabitation has become more prevalent alongside the decrease in marriage since the 1970s. Although nothing new, as social historians are keen to point out, the difference is that it began to be carried out much more openly from the 1970s onwards and became much more accepted. Whereas only 3 per cent of all adult women were openly cohabiting in 1979, this figure had risen to 13 per cent by 1998. One in seven families, defined as parents and at least one child, were unmarried but officially registered as parents of their joint children in 2006.

Among the Sixty Somethings, around four in ten had been in long-term relationships or marriages of up to 40 years, often from a young age and with a first live-in partner. A few of these women were somewhat self-deprecating. Betty, married since 1972, said 'I'm a very boring person,' while Robin described herself as 'a married and faithful wife' and 'boring'. Elizabeth called herself 'very dull'. She'd met her husband three weeks after they'd arrived at university as teenagers, lived with him for a while but wed at 22 before they had children. As she said, 'you pick the right person in the first place and the rest is easy.' 'I'm a great one for taking my husband for granted ... I think there are some things you should take for granted,' she added.

Most of the 67 women had been married at some time, but the timing, and the events precipitating their marriages, were very different. Some had been fairly rapid affairs. Jo, who had been married over 40 years, stands out in this respect as she and her husband had decided to stay together on the very evening they met. They'd got a special licence the next day and were married within ten days. Jo said they 'just got on with it' because they were both on the move and were worried they might split up otherwise. The special licence cost £4, their wedding rings were £4 each and the whole thing cost £12. They were both 23 at the time and married in their lunch hour. Her son in his mid-twenties had told her that she and her husband had made life impossible for him and her sister by setting the bar so high in terms of falling in love. Others had got married young, even if not so precipitously. Hannah had left school at 18 and decided not to go to university as she wanted to get married, as had Sarah. Hannah's marriage was still ongoing, but Sarah's had ended after four years.

Sometimes pressures, especially from families, had precipitated marriage. Alice said she'd got married young because she didn't want to feel her mother regarded her as she regarded other people who 'lived in sin' or had sex without being married. As it turned out, it was a waste of effort as her mother never actually liked her husband anyway. Lois had decided to get married and 'fixed it all up in a few days' so that she and her partner could move into a flat owned by her parents. They hadn't anywhere to live and had been told they had to get married if they wanted it. Sometimes pregnancy was the factor rushing Sixty Somethings into marriage. Lindyloo hadn't wanted to get married but was under pressure to do so when she found she was expecting a baby. That marriage had lasted ten years. Jan, who had met her husband at 15 and married him upon becoming pregnant at 19, had by contrast remained in the relationship. 'Despite a shotgun marriage ... we're still together,' she said. Others, such as Mary and Rachel, both of whom hadn't wanted to live together unmarried, had met at university and wed shortly after graduation. Skelton too married her boyfriend when they both came to the end of their studying. They would be moving away otherwise, and 'it seemed to be the thing to do at that age'.

Practical rather than romantic reasons were often the impetus for marriage taking place after a considerable period of cohabitation. Regularising tax matters, sometimes in relation to health issues, was mentioned by Geraldine, Jude, Melissa, Sarah and Winifred. Beth had moved in with her husband when she was in her very early twenties, but it was 19 years before they got married. There were seven people at their wedding, including their children. Women didn't always go into these marriages lightly. As Geraldine said, 'I did feel it required a justification. For so many of us, we made a statement about living together.' Winifred, who'd met her current husband in 1975, taken his surname and had children, didn't marry until some thirty years later. She was glad they had, but it 'didn't matter' to her.

Women had yet other reasons for getting married. Lynne had wed because she and her husband planned to adopt, although in fact they never did, and Eleanor had done so because her husband felt it was an important statement to make. Katherine's wedding occurred when she was seven months pregnant and she came back to the UK with a German partner threatened with deportation. It was a 'shotgun marriage with a shotgun firmly in my back'. Primrose had been married twice, first to a Polish man to allow him to stay in the UK and second to a gay nurse to allow her to remain longer in Australia with her female partner. She never divorced this second husband.

Even in their adult years, some women were still exposed to influences from their parents when it came to matters of marriage and morality. Melissa married after 30 years of cohabitation, but separated three years later. She says her mother never forgave her for not getting married sooner and hid the wedding photo Melissa had given her. She didn't want to tell people her daughter hadn't been married before. In Theresa's case, it had been disapproval from the mother of her second husband-to-be when coming to stay with her. Despite cohabiting with him, her putative mother-in-law had told her 'of course, you don't have to sleep in the same bed.' As Theresa said, 'Well, that wasn't going to happen, so blow that for a lark.' Alison had bought a flat with her husband before they married, but they were put in separate bedrooms when they went home. On one occasion her mother had to put them together because other people were staying. 'I'm going to put you two in together but I'm not going to bring you tea in the morning,' she'd said. So that's where she drew the line. A somewhat different issue faced Poppy, who didn't change her name on marriage. This had gone down incredibly badly in her husband's family, but it was only about 15 years later that his mother had said she thought it had been illegal. They had seen Poppy's decision as a personal rejection, whereas for her it was a feminist statement.

Relationships and marriages do of course go wrong, and four in ten of the women overall had been divorced at some point. This may be a slightly higher rate than in the population as a whole. Official statistics suggest that one in five marriages taking place in 1968 had ended in divorce within 15 years and that one in three marriages in 1998 had ended over a similar period. Violet said she didn't know many people in her age group who weren't divorced. Couples ran out of steam in relationships and moved on to the next, she suggested. Dolly, however, was the first person in her extended family to get divorced.

For some Sixty Somethings the point of divorce had come very early on. Helen said she'd known her first marriage was a mistake from the outset, and had already broken off the engagement once. However, her mother had managed to persuade her it was just cold feet. She had never been very happy about it but felt 'I had made my bed and must lie on it come what may, even before I was married to him. I felt morally bound by my commitment, even though I was very young.' However, things came to a head when she'd had a 'very intense' relationship with someone else. She then left her husband and instigated divorce, upsetting and angering her parents. Frances too had wanted to get away from her first husband for years and years but then ended up having two children with him. 'It is beyond understanding,' she said. Molly had got married at 21 'because I thought you had to' and remarried in her late twenties 'because I still thought you had to be married'. She met her current partner after a second divorce but will not get married again. Jane too had quite a brief marriage at a young age, leaving it when it was apparent it wasn't working. 'I always thought I would remarry but it didn't happen … It never happened that anyone seemed right,' she said. Lynne's first marriage had been 'a disaster' and lasted only six months.

Sometimes it seemed marriages had been actively abusive. One woman, describing her marriage as 'horrible', said she now realised she'd been in an 'abusive and emotionally controlling relationship'. She had met her husband when she was very young and felt she'd missed out on her teenage years. When she walked out of the marriage she didn't ever want to speak to a man again. She did, however, later remarry. Another had met her husband when she was 14 and he was the first person she ever kissed. They went out for about a year and 'he was very sweet then', she said. When they got back together when she was 22, she thought she was marrying the same sweet 14-year-old. However, it emerged that he had had an affair with an older woman in the meanwhile and been introduced to 'perverse sex parties and stuff'. Eventually, and perhaps inevitably, the relationship floundered when she discovered his infidelity, but only after several decades raising a family together. Another, who referred to her husband as 'the bastard', said she'd had an 'awful relationship'. After her divorce, she had nothing except a handful of silver cutlery, two pictures, two chairs and a mattress. Before she left him, her husband gave her a small cheque in a restaurant and announced to everyone present that she was leaving him, to her and their embarrassment. He made her sign something in front of them to say she wouldn't take any more. She said she was 'so passive that I didn't contest his behaviour'.

Other marriages broke up for different reasons. Skelton said 'we just agreed we didn't want to live together any more. There were no catastrophic events.' She'd read an article which she thought explained a lot. This suggested that testosterone goes up during the menopause, causing women to take a matter-of-fact approach and decide not to put up with things they're not happy about. She saw it as 'a bit of a medical condition'. Clara, who hadn't wanted her marriage to end when it did, had come to the point when she thought 'whose life is it anyway?' She and her husband had wanted very different things and it was not working out. For Dolly it was different yet again. She and her husband had grown up together and she'd never expected to divorce. She commented how the 'male midlife crisis was alive and well' and how it is possible to sleepwalk in long relationships.

Most Sixty Somethings had been married, but there were seven who had never had a husband or civil partner. This was usually from choice. 'I have avoided marriage because I've never ever felt the need. I've been asked three times, but I've never seen the point,' said Lilian. She had, however, got very close to it on one occasion when she and her current partner were thinking they might get married for pension purposes. They had booked the register office but cancelled when her partner's father became ill and they worried he might die the day before the wedding.

They never made alternative plans. Audrey too said she would never for a moment have considered getting married. She'd been extremely unhappy as she grew up and had no wish to create another nuclear family. Her own political ideas and her views on feminism also made it an anathema. Meg, who had always been single, was intensely independent. She'd had significant relationships, the most important of which was with someone who was married. She'd had no illusions and liked it as it was. Miranda, who'd cohabited with various people, for up to seven years, was 'now happily single'.

Tabitha, whose partner had died two years earlier, had never been formally married. 'Marriage would never have suited me,' she said. Stephanie also believed in the importance of cohabitation, having taken 35 years to marry her husband. She talked about the 'ridiculous thing about being a virgin' when you get married. Having been a couples counsellor, she sees the importance of being free from that rigid thinking. Barbara tended to agree, saying she approved of cohabitation and would never have married her first husband if she'd lived with him first.

Some women who had been married in the past would not consider doing it again. For Hazel Grace, it was a 'feminist thing'. She had believed in marriage when much younger, partly in reaction to her parents' unusual views on marriage and fidelity, but had now decided 'I don't mate in captivity'. Others did not feel constrained by convention as they got older and saw themselves as free to conduct their relationships as it suited them. Molly, for instance, talked about her current relationship, which had already lasted 20 years and was the best she'd ever had. She and her partner had lived together for only the past three years, but even then it was not full-time cohabitation as he lived independently upstairs during the week but came downstairs at weekends when they were together. Persia, who had had a long-term partner for some thirty years until he died, told how they both kept their own houses but got together from Friday to Monday. She said it worked brilliantly for them but would never have happened in her parents' generation.

Attitudes to monogamy in relationships were mixed. A number of women suggested faithfulness was extremely important to them. Mary believed in lifelong commitment, and although Tweegy didn't mind 'playing around a little bit' before marriage, she strongly favoured stable monogamous relationships afterwards. Monogamy was not, however, always a key ingredient of the marriages that lasted. One of the women said she hadn't been entirely faithful to her husband, although she thought he had been faithful to her. They'd made an agreement early on that they could have other partners if they wanted to, but that they wouldn't tell each other. 'I don't have this possessive feeling and never did,' she said. Another Sixty Something said she and her husband had 'sneaky affairs when younger', all confessed or found out, adding that 'it was only sex, for goodness' sake'. It could be miserable and terribly destructive, she thought, but 'it' shouldn't break a marriage up. After all, she and her husband had stayed together. Other women indicated that they had not always had exclusive sexual relationships, with Sylvie saying she'd always had affairs and other relationships during her marriage, as had her husband. But they had been 'terribly happy together' and they would never have got divorced or split the family home.

On the other hand, several women mentioned how affairs had broken up their marriages. Hayley said in her case it was the 'my husband ran off with my best friend scenario'. He'd put her down quite a lot when they'd been together and she'd been shocked when he left to find that 'quite a lot of people' thought she was 'quite nice'. She said she slept with 'quite a lot of them' for about six months until she got bored. 'I was a real pushover,' she said.

Others questioned how far open marriages and relationships could really be successful. Ruby, for one, recalled a period when there was a lot more experimentation going on and she had been in an open relationship with a long-term partner. With hindsight, she believed it an illusion that you could have affairs without terribly hurting a partner's feelings. Even though she and her partner at the time had agreed they would experiment, they hadn't been able to keep their relationship together 'because we weren't sophisticated enough to be separating out these different relationships and feelings'. She added that, 'It's not what I want now. And I got my fingers burned. It didn't do anybody any good.' Lilian similarly told of an open relationship she'd had many years ago, concluding that she was 'not sure it was entirely wise in retrospect'. Problems arose if 'something serious was going on' and one partner fell in love. That created jealousy that could spoil the central relationship. In Maureen's view, free love was not all it was cracked up to be.

Over half the Sixty Somethings were on at least their second serious relationship and had met their current partner well into their adulthood. Dating sites had proved successful in a number of cases. Encouraged by their daughters, both Verity and Skelton had found partners in this way. Skelton said she hadn't really been looking for another partner and felt quite uncomfortable being posted on the dating site. She didn't make any contacts herself but her profile attracted one response. The compatibility match was given as 100 per cent so she decided to meet. The first date was a success and 'so that was that really'. They moved in together as 'we're getting too old to mess about. Time's not on our side any more.' Hazel Grace had also been successful in meeting her current partner in this way and said she would try again should anything happen to him. 'I like being with someone so I'd instantly try to find someone. I'd be out dating even in my seventies or eighties … I'm quite easily pleased. I'm not tremendously picky,' she said. Ruby too had met her husband through a lonely hearts column when she was 45. While she had been a bit secretive about it at the time, she noted how attitudes had changed and that it's now easy to be open about having met on a dating site. Winifred and Molly also mentioned meeting partners through dating sites, but Helen had tried this route with less luck. She had met two men through Guardian Soulmates when she'd been on her own for a brief time and recalled meeting the first in a restaurant with her friend loitering nearby to make sure everything was okay. He'd been a huge believer in astrology and, for her, that was that. Her second meeting was again unpromising.

One enormous change over the lifetime of the Sixty Somethings has been in attitudes towards homosexuality. Although sexual relationships between women have never been illegal, men engaging in relationships with men were, until the Sexual Offences Act 1967, punishable by a prison sentence. Subsequent years saw legislation allowing gay people to join the armed forces and to adopt children. This was followed by the Civil Partnership Act 2004 and the Marriage (Same Sex Couples) Act 2013. Prior to the 2013 Act, the Equality Act 2010 made discrimination on the basis of sexual orientation illegal.

The Sixty Somethings acknowledged this major change, some saying they hadn't known anybody who was gay, or at least hadn't known they were gay, as they grew up. It seemed to be something that was not talked about. By contrast, Chenhalls thought that most educated people in her generation now believe in gender equality and are against homophobia. Melissa suggested her generation might have benefited from the current fluidity in sexuality.

While 64 of the 67 women identified as exclusively heterosexual, three did not. Jacca, Primrose and Katherine had all had both male and female relationships, and Katherine was mother to a son. Jacca had had a civil partnership with a woman she lived with for 25 years until her death, and Primrose had twice been married to men she did not have relationships with. Primrose came out as a lesbian at the age of 27 and said, 'I call myself bisexual although I haven't had a relationship with a man for 40 years ... I would have said I was drawn to women.' She had grown up with a lot of sexual guilt in the context of a strict Christian upbringing. Jacca, by contrast, didn't define herself as gay and still doesn't. She explained that this wasn't a political statement, that it was much more fluid than that. She felt it's possible to fall in love with anyone and 'whatever sort of genitals they had didn't seem to be particularly relevant'. She felt out on a limb and didn't really fit anywhere. She'd been waiting for the world to catch up with her, 'which it finally has'. Katherine described how her first passion in life was for another girl at school. She wondered why it had taken her so long to come out.

Becoming parents

Eight in ten of the Sixty Somethings were mothers. Among these, three-fifths had given birth to two children, with three the next most common number, followed by one, four and, in one case, five. Seven women had stepchildren or an adopted child, usually in addition to their own biological children, and some mothers had children with more than one father. Two children had died since birth.

The proportion of Sixty Somethings with children couldn't be compared with the proportion in their parents' generation as all their parents had, by definition, had children. Some comparison can, however, be made on family size. Whereas two was by far the most common number of children for the Sixty Somethings, two or three children were equally common in the older generation. There were also twice as many families with a single child in the older generation as in the younger, and two families in the older, but none in the younger, with six children. There was also a greater prevalence of step-, half- and adopted children in the younger generation than the older.

Official statistics also point to change over time. Women born in 1925, a typical birth year for the Sixty Somethings' parents, were more likely to have had children than those born in 1945, although childlessness decreased somewhat again beyond this point. For those born in 1945 and 1955 the population percentages of women without children were around 10 and 16 per cent respectively. This is a slightly lower figure than that found for the Sixty Somethings. There had also been a decline in larger families from 1935, with two-child families being the most common at all dates. In line with these trends, the Sixty Somethings tended to have fewer children than their mothers.

The child-rearing climate when the Sixty Somethings were bringing up their own children had also changed markedly from their own childhood days. If Truby King and Dr Spock influenced how they were brought up, then Penelope Leach was a significant figure when they themselves became parents. Selling more than two million copies of *Your Baby and Child: From Birth to Age Five*, published in 1977, Penelope Leach advocated a style of parenting that was child-centred and avoided rules and routines for their own sake. She advised parents to listen to both their child and themselves and work out what to do that is in everyone's best interests. She was against smacking and saw the happiness of both mother and child as paramount. The importance of one-to-one care was stressed and, while the main focus was on mothers, there was acknowledgement of the significance of the paternal role.

This change in emphasis came through loud and clear from the Sixty Somethings, most of whom stressed how differently they had brought up their own children compared to how they had been brought up themselves. Their children were the centre of their families in a way that they hadn't been, said Alice, while many others suggested they felt closer to their children than they'd felt, or still felt, to their own parents. One key difference seemed to be the relative ease of communication and the topics that were on and off bounds. Frances, for example, says she talks openly to her children but edits massively when talking to her mother. Elizabeth similarly indicated that she's quite guarded with her mother because there is so much she doesn't approve of. For instance, she never told her that she'd lived with her husband before they got married. Charlotte too said that she was different with her children than her parents had been with her. 'They can talk to me about anything, really,' she said. Sex had been a particularly taboo subject in the older generations, but there were others too. Dolly's grandfather would never have sex, religion or politics discussed at the dinner table as he said it upset the meal and made for indigestion.

Indeed, sometimes there seemed little restraint in what their children told the Sixty Somethings. Alison said her son's girlfriend got out and took her contraceptive pill in the kitchen, with no secrecy at all, and Jenny said her son came down to tell her after he'd lost his virginity in their house. Sometimes there's 'too much information', she said. Barbara's daughter had also told her mother when she'd lost her virginity, somewhat upsetting her in the process, as well as when she had haemorrhoids. Barbara wasn't at all sure she'd have told her own mother similar things. She was much more open with her children but still wouldn't tell them everything, such as if she goes on a date. Verity was the first person her daughter talked to about contraception.

Not only the child-rearing climate but also the women's own experiences during the sixties and seventies were seen as contributing to the changed relationships between parents and their children. 'All that openness helped us talk to our children better,' suggested Lynne, while Jenny said she was 'determined to bring up a confident but emotionally intelligent son, and I think I have'. Maureen thought her generation was more tolerant of children's little rebellions because they had been through rebellions themselves. She said she and her husband had discussed how they were going to bring up their children and had decided they were going to be tolerant, but not too lenient. She mentioned Philip Larkin's poem 'This Be the Verse', first published in 1971, which they didn't want to emulate. As many Sixty Somethings were aware, the first verse of the poem is:

> They fuck you up, your mum and dad.
> They may not mean to, but they do.
> They fill you with the faults they had
> And add some extra, just for you.

With greater openness had come greater acceptance and valuing of individuality. Among the women were those with children who were gay, transgender or had become Muslim. These children's orientations and decisions were viewed positively. Maggie, who said she'd originally had two daughters with her second husband but now has one daughter and one son as the youngest has changed gender, said, 'We got there pretty quickly ... He's still exactly the same person.' She and her son had just recorded a conversation for the *Listening Project* on Radio 4. 'So our family is not completely conventional,' she said.

Although Clara felt there was more of a feeling of togetherness in families in the past, most of the Sixty Somethings thought otherwise and talked about their greater involvement in their children's lives and how they enjoy doing things with them. The Sixty Somethings, in fact, were more likely to identify with 'This Be the Worst', Adrian Mitchell's parody of the Larkin poem:

> They tuck you up, your mum and dad,
> They read you Peter Rabbit, too.
> They give you all the treats they had
> And add some extra, just for you.

At the same time, many felt their children were far more dependent on them, emotionally and financially, than they had been on their parents. Many communicated on a regular basis through WhatsApp groups, email or telephone, and were in almost daily contact. Alison outlined the benefits of keeping in touch as finding out what they're up to and making them realise that parents aren't just the boring older generation. 'We're not completely foreign beings to them,' said Violet. This view was endorsed by Elizabeth, who contrasted her knowledge of her children with that of her parents. 'Our parents had no idea what it was like – the way we lived, our lives as students. It was a complete mystery,' she said.

The Sixty Somethings as a whole did, nonetheless, have some reservations about parenting in their generation. Persia suggested that children had become much more cosseted, that they were more 'precious' than when she was young. The women had talked about the freedom and independence they'd enjoyed in their childhood, but there was a feeling that subsequent generations hadn't been allowed to do all the same things. Alison thought this protection, as well as the constant praise, had perhaps gone too far. She commented how young people could struggle to cope with being criticised at work. Rachel suggested that perhaps they had been wrong in being loving indulgent parents who found it hard to set limits and boundaries, making their children take longer to grow up and settle down. On the other hand, she thought the present-day economic situation, the sense of entitlement of Thatcher children growing up in the 'me' generation and a possible feeling of there being more time because of increased life expectancy, might also be playing a part. Others commented on how their children's generation was more materialistic than theirs had been.

Annie told how her generation had brought up their children to question things more than they had ever done. Theresa illustrated this change in her own family. She'd implemented a rule that her children could ask 'why' only six times but then that was it. Her father had asked her why she didn't just tell them 'because I said so' as she had been told as a child. She saw that as a very clear change in values, authority and respect. Whereas she didn't see asking questions as a lack of respect, her father did. Eleanor said that children now don't seem to worry about swearing in front of their parents, which could be seen as making a similar point.

Melissa's son summed up what he saw as the difference in how his and his parents' generations had been brought up. He'd told her, 'Your parents' generation didn't have particularly high expectations for you. So you were very lucky because things went much better than you might have expected. You more than exceeded any expectations they may have had. And the big difference is now in our generation, you gave us high expectations. And of course we've all struggled like mad and we're never going to fulfil them.'

Although most of the Sixty Somethings had children, around one in five did not. For some this was a conscious choice, while for others it was down to personal circumstances, including an inability to have them. Also, while some women seemed quite happy with their childless state, others appeared to have regrets. For instance, Molly had never wished she'd had children of her own and Hayley, who was unable to have them, said she was not particularly maternal. On the other hand, Jemima had found being childless hard to come to terms with. Several women without children pointed to their strong relationships with other family members, such as nephews and nieces. Ruby said that 'family is really really important to me', pointing out that she didn't consider children as the only family who matter. She had brothers, their children and cousins, and had very close relationships with all of them. Jane also pointed out how people who are single and don't have children are useful because they have more time to help others.

Most of these women recognised that their lives would have been different had they become mothers. Stella suggested that not having children meant greater isolation and less opportunity to be in touch with younger people, and Lissa suggested she was 'much more selfish and self-centred' as a result. Several wondered who would be looking out for them as they got older. Jacca had worried about her mother and whether she was safe, and thought it partly a relief that nobody had to do that for her. But it was also quite a strange experience and a scary place to be when something went wrong. 'I haven't got kids ringing me. I phoned my mother every day for 20 years,' she said, adding that she doesn't feel hard done by. Stella too pointed to the two sides of the picture. She thought that being childless meant losing out on a lot of joy people with children have, and lacking a certain maturity 'because I've not had children questioning me', but that, on the other hand, 'you don't have that worry, what are they doing, are they happy, are they unhappy ... you can't walk away from that.'

Employment

Patterns of employment, especially for women, were rapidly changing at the time the Sixty Somethings were leaving education or training and looking for work. The Institute for Employment Studies (IES) has shown how, from the mid-seventies to the mid-nineties, the proportion of women in paid jobs rose from considerably less than 60 per cent to over 70 per cent. Notable at this time was also the increased likelihood for mothers to work so that by 1992, those with children were more likely than not to work. Indeed, the rate of female employment among those with children under the age of five rose from a quarter to 43 per cent between 1973 and 1992. Much of this increase was due to women in part-time employment. Unemployment was also relatively low at this time, and at a quarter of the rate in the 1980s. It is therefore unsurprising that, unlike in their mothers' generation, all the Sixty Somethings worked for many of their adult years. Many took time off when their children were small, or changed course to something more compatible with their family roles, but employment was nonetheless significant within all of their lives.

Jobs were plentiful at the time. You could walk out of a job on Friday and into another on Monday, said Dolly. This sentiment was echoed by many others. 'We always took it for granted we could find a job,' said Barbara, while Tweegy didn't know any of her contemporaries who didn't get the jobs they wanted. She didn't think there had been any great anxiety about finding work. Ruby had stopped working for six months when she was in her late twenties and hadn't thought anything of it. Moreover, there were opportunities for all. Carol pointed to the lack of emphasis on grades and educational qualifications. 'Even if you didn't do so well in O levels, as they were then, you could still find a job somewhere ... there would still be opportunities for you.' For those who went into public sector professions, such as the civil service or education, there were also worthwhile pensions.

Expectations about women working were also changing. Many parents were keen for their daughters to have the opportunities they had missed, and the women themselves also usually wanted to work. 'I found all my confidence and self-esteem outside the home ... massively, massively,' said Tabitha. Annie said there was a feeling that their housewife mothers had been deprived in some way and that her generation wanted a job they could enjoy and that brought in money they could spend as they liked. 'I had to earn a living. For me everything is about not being bored,' said Jane.

Traditional attitudes nonetheless still prevailed to a certain degree. Many women said their parents supported them in finding work but expected them to stop once they had their own families. This wasn't what many of the women expected to do. They might take a break while their children were small, but they planned to resume work afterwards. It was, for instance, a huge shock to Jan's family when she decided to pursue her career. Her husband earned well and she didn't have to work, but she wanted to. Geraldine's mother too was upset that her daughter had rejected her way of life. 'I never ever ever ever wanted to be the stay-at-home mother. I just thought it was the worst most vulnerable position to be in and I just couldn't bear it,' said Geraldine.

It had indeed been considered odd, by most of her contemporaries, and certainly by her parents, that Chenhalls had wanted to continue working after her first child. Olive said her mother had told her, 'I wouldn't have your life. I couldn't have brought up children and been as involved in work as you are.' However, it was what the majority of the Sixty Somethings did. As Annie pointed out, husbands were often in favour as they realised they could get a better home if both partners were working.

Nonetheless, many women did feel a sense of conflict, and Alison said that the majority of women she knew had expected to look after their own children, for a while at least, and she had only one friend who went back to work full-time. Most of her female acquaintances didn't work again until their children were about five years old. The shortage of part-time jobs and under-regulated childcare helped women reach this decision. The most straightforward conclusion, which applied to Alison herself, was to stay at home when there was a small child to look after.

Most of the Sixty Somethings who became mothers did much the same, stopping work for a while but going back later. This wasn't always easy. Barbara felt guilty when she returned to work but reasoned that she would feel miserable and resentful if she gave up her job, and Helen was torn her whole working life as she found it hard to leave her children. Sarah too pointed to the dilemma between work and motherhood, and Mary said, 'I cannot square for myself what ought to happen about women and work.' As Olive pointed out, class is a key factor to be taken into account, as it is almost impossible to stay at home to look after your children unless you have a well-paid husband.

Going back to work also created other difficulties. For Betty it was being 'on the back foot' after time out, having to take time off work for the children and ending up with more housework and childcare to fit in. The original OXO family advertisement that ran during the sixties until 1976, with Katie, Philip and their baby son, epitomised the perfect housewife – even if she did blot her copybook in one episode by making gravy without first washing her hands. Shirley Conran also published *Superwoman: Every Woman's Book of Household Management* in 1975, at a time when many of the Sixty Somethings were busy juggling their lives. One of the straplines on the cover of the book claims it will give away secrets on 'how to be a working wife and mother'. Conran didn't make it all sound easy, but she did suggest it could be managed. There was a lot to live up to. As Julia said, a woman had to work and be a homemaker. Frances added that you had to be a superwoman 'and be a great lover and look brilliant'. And for many, such as Jo, domestic life was ultimately more important, despite a good career.

The jobs the Sixty Somethings had over their working lives were many and various. Teaching of one kind or another, from infants to university students to adult learners, dominated their professions, and health and welfare, broadly defined, came second. Here there were women who might have become a GP, nurse, social worker, community worker, counsellor, clinical and educational psychologist, physiotherapist, masseur, therapist, probation officer, manager of a youth project or support worker. Other careers were as academic, researcher, actor, journalist, creative writer, garden maintenance worker, civil servant, librarian, secretary or personal assistant, administrator, magistrate, musician, farmer, businesswoman, furniture maker, publisher, art dealer, consultant, fashion buyer, fundraiser, charity worker, organiser of educational tours, medical artist, barrister, advertising and marketing worker, developer of training materials, public relations officer, landlady, technician, systems engineer and information technologist. Jobs also mentioned by the women, usually undertaken on a short-term basis, included estate agent, temping, running a shop, sales assistant, dental receptionist, lavatory lady, importer of china and tableware, air stewardess, waitress, box office assistant, clerk in an insurance company and bank, milk roundswoman, cleaner and petrol pump attendant.

Barbara suggested that while some of her peers became high-powered business executives, most of the women she knew were not interested in that type of job and went for those considered more 'socially responsible'. In part this reflected the ideological mood of the generation, and in part the changing employment market. The IES report demonstrated how the two decades from the 1970s saw a significant rise in the service sector accompanying a decline in manufacturing, with women disproportionately taking up the available jobs. Another marked change during this period was women's entry into professional and managerial employment. Whereas just 12 per cent of women were in these occupations in 1971, the corresponding proportion by 1993 was 20 per cent. Lois pointed to this growth in service-type careers and the large number of women who worked in public institutions and got jobs for life. 'We only wanted working roles that were ideologically right,' said Jenny, while Meg had wanted something interesting, of social value, and that paid the bills. 'I've been very lucky that that's been exactly how it's worked out,' she said.

Paying the bills, rather than earning as much as they could, seemed important for many Sixty Somethings. Robin herself always wanted to do something she enjoyed, not necessarily something that would earn her the most money, and Geraldine told how she had lots of friends in public sector jobs who had steered clear of working for the commercial sector. They had wanted jobs they could be proud of, that were important and mattered. They'd accepted they wouldn't make as much money as if they'd gone into a career such as banking, but they did nonetheless expect pensions at the end. 'I wanted to make enough money, but didn't want more money than I needed,' added Alice.

A number of the women talked about working in male-dominated settings, and for the most part spoke of this favourably. Elizabeth had always worked with men, teaching science. 'I was in charge of them, so I quite liked that,' she said. Robin and Persia had both worked in a male environment in the information technology sector. Robin thought it was great, particularly as women have different skills and so in many ways had more opportunities and got on better than some male colleagues. Persia also enjoyed her work and remarked on how the company she was with for many years was very good at looking after women. She did, however, tell the story of being awarded a tiepin as a recognition of achievement. When she mentioned that she didn't wear a tie, it was suggested she might go for a second award so that she could have two tiepins to have made into a pair of earrings.

Sarah's experience in a government department was also male-dominated. She was one of very few women not doing clerical jobs and did admit there were 'a few mountains to climb there', but she loved her job and 'couldn't wait to get to work in the morning'. Tabitha, employed in advertising, marketing and PR, said that the places she worked were often 'bastions of sexism' but that she just found it funny. She'd worked in some industries, notably brewing, where there weren't any women at all. However, she said she never noticed it and never had any trouble getting on. She was also the youngest female director of a company at one point. Admitting that it was a sweeping generalisation, she said she'd probably thought that if you sat around complaining that you didn't get a job because you were a woman, you probably weren't suitable for the job anyway. 'I just got on and did it,' she remarked. Lilian on the other hand, who had sometimes been the only woman tutoring 20 men, said she felt she spent the eighties 'challenging sexism, racism and homophobia'.

The women were divided when it came to their experiences of opportunities and pay for men and women. Although civil service reforms in the UK in 1956 had given men and women in

government jobs the right to equal pay, financial discrimination was still in evidence. The IES report had also shown how women on average earned more than a third less than men in 1970, but four-fifths as much by 1994. Some improvements were brought about by the Equal Pay Act 1970 and the Sex Discrimination Act 1975 that, among other things, aimed to ensure that working conditions and training were the same for all employees. The fact that men and women were not similarly represented in different types of employment contributed to the continuation of a glass ceiling.

Some Sixty Somethings, especially those in teaching and civil service jobs, generally felt they were paid the same as men, but this was far from true for everyone. Helen, for instance, was appalled to find she was paid less than anyone else at a major bank, and Winifred said there were always more jobs for actors than actresses. Audrey had twice taken action on her own behalf to gain equal pay to men similarly employed, and had been successful in both cases. She thought this had been easier in the public sector, where things were more transparent. Certainly, there seemed enormous differences depending on the setting. Jemima thought there had probably been equity in pay within the teaching profession but had been surprised by the differences when she worked as a tomato-picker one summer. The men had earned four shillings and sixpence an hour but the women, who she said worked harder than the men, only three shillings and elevenpence. Jemima had got four shillings and twopence and thought this was because she knew the owner.

Pay was but one area in which Sixty Somethings could be at a disadvantage. Motherhood could also present difficulties. The Employment Protection Act introduced statutory maternity pay and job reinstatement rights, but several women who wanted to go back to work part-time after the birth of their first child found they were unable to do so. Sarah was a case in point. She'd found motherhood 'a bit scary' to start with and 'a bit of a shock to the system'. Women didn't generally go back to work after having a child and there was no provision for flexibility and part-time work. She went back and 'ended up doing two jobs badly – one in the office and one at home'. She eventually managed to negotiate part-time work for eighteen months. At the time she wrote a paper outlining how it would be better for all if women could have long career breaks. She said it was 'reviewed by twelve blokes around a table and they all laughed'. Helen also faced opposition to returning to work part-time after she'd had a baby, and left the bank she was working at after four years, a year short of the five she needed for a pension. Elizabeth had resigned provisionally from her job when pregnant, which meant she could keep the job if the baby died. That was in 1977 and, following the Employment Protection Act, the first year that had been possible.

Sexism was encountered in other ways too. Both Annie and Helen had been told they couldn't wear trousers at work, and Barbara said she'd got bunions from the obligatory high heels. Hayley reported how the office she worked in used to give flowers to the women if they'd done a good job. She managed to persuade the boss to give vouchers instead to anyone who deserved them. On other occasions sexism was more implicit. Poppy for example had been annoyed by a meeting she'd gone to with a junior and male colleague who was assumed to be her boss.

Not many women suggested that positive discrimination had worked in their favour. However, Lilian did. She believed she had got a particular job over other candidates who were almost certainly more experienced. 'Some eyebrows were raised,' but she had no problem with what had happened. It was needed to break male domination, she said. Betty also said she'd been very lucky at work with a forward-looking boss. She was promoted and given responsibility and never came up against 'no, you can't do something'. Her bosses wanted to be seen as supporting feminism.

Direct sexual harassment was also mentioned, although only occasionally. On one memorable occasion for Primrose, in a bench job for a joinery manufacturer and the only woman on the shop floor, she started getting a hard time from the men in the paint shop because of a relationship she was having with a younger woman. She had returned from holiday and found a picture of an enormous penis waiting for her with the words 'Sit on this you bitch'. She tore it down and told her boss she wasn't putting up with it. He tried to persuade her to stay but she walked out. Soon after, another woman had a similar experience, went to court and was awarded £13,000.

Money, money, money

All Sixty Somethings earned money from paid employment during the course of their lives, but this did not necessarily give them equality. Although, as Hayley pointed out, having money in their own right offered women more of a chance to lead alternative lifestyles and get divorced, there were also obstacles in the way. Until the Sex Discrimination Act 1975, during the years of early adulthood for the women, discrimination on the grounds of sex and marriage was still lawful. Many Sixty Somethings recalled occasions in which they had personally been disadvantaged. Jemima, for instance, was told she could have a mortgage as a married woman only if the form was signed by her husband. Meg also pointed to this requirement, and

Tweegy told how a wife's income was not taken into account for mortgages as it was assumed she was going to have babies. Molly said she'd had to put her husband down as the main breadwinner on an insurance form even though she had a professional job herself.

The 1975 legislation was a landmark change for women. Margaret thought the most important driver for female equality was probably getting a salary cheque in your own bank account. In Betty's view, allowing women to enter contracts on their own was also critical. She remembered ripping up a hire purchase contract when she was told her husband had to sign it. 'I suppose that was non-conformity in a way,' she said. Another woman pointed to the problems she'd had in stopping her then husband from draining their bank account, as his signature was required for anything to be done. Frances had also suffered from the inequality embedded in the law when she'd got divorced. Her ex-husband had paid her maintenance and a small amount of alimony, but she had to pay tax on it while he got tax relief.

The introduction of credit cards to the UK in the early 1970s, of which the first was Barclaycard, also had some impact. These were not actively targeted at women until 1973, although they had existed for some five years by that time, but they struck a new note in that a woman did not need a male guarantor to sign her application.

The changes in law and practice no doubt contributed to the changed status of women across the generations as well as their attitudes to money. Jacca said her mother had had her life imposed on her because she had no financial independence, no qualifications and because of the culture. Several other women also pointed to how their mothers had been trapped in unhappy marriages because they had no means of escape. There had been major shifts in all these respects for the Sixty Somethings. Persia neatly illustrated how having and spending money had evolved over the generations in her family. Her grandmother had had to rely totally on her grandfather for money, as her mother had had to rely on her father. However, her parents, unlike her grandparents, had had a joint account which meant her mother could buy what she wanted even though she would discuss it with her husband first. Persia, however, was totally financially independent and would, if she wanted something, 'just go and buy it'.

There remained, nonetheless, a divide between the sexes. Although many women had achieved financial independence, Carol suggested that men were still generally the breadwinners among her contemporaries. She had only one male friend who chose to do most of the childcare and let his wife work long hours. Flavia recalled the expectation that men should be the ones to bring in the money. For Zena, the decision was a pragmatic one. Her husband could earn three times what she could earn, and so: 'I manage the money, he just earns it.'

Among the women as a whole, however, there were a few who had taken on the role of main breadwinner. Lilian, Liza and Stella were among these, and Jo had been the only earner for a while when her husband had stopped working to look after the children. She pointed out how he had generally been fine about this 'role reversal' but sometimes got upset because he didn't have any money of his own. As she pointed out, this was similar to how many women had felt in the past. Hazel Grace had always been the breadwinner in her marriage, but now her younger partner earns more. 'I think that's an achievement to have a toy boy who supports you financially,' she said.

The greater wealth experienced by families as they moved through the 1970s and 1980s, brought about by the economic boom, women's employment, fewer children and other factors, led to changed patterns of spending over the adult years of the Sixty Somethings. The finances of the women varied and fluctuated but there was, in general, an upward trend. Frances commented on how things had changed from the 1950s when everything was mended and passed on to the conspicuous consumption she had witnessed as her generation had got older. Flavia illustrated changes by noting the differences between when she was a student in the sixties and in the nineties. On the first occasion she had lived in a primitive flat, whereas by the later date she was accommodated in a student flat equipped with a washing machine and other modern equipment.

Some women had indeed suffered considerable hardship as they'd embarked on their adult lives. Lindyloo was among many who recalled how she'd started out with everything second-hand and no expectation of anything new, and Eleanor talked about the very basic lifestyle she'd led. They hadn't had much money, stuffing up gaps in the windows with newspaper when it was cold and rushing home at lunchtime to tend to the washing. She remembered running out of money when all they had in the house were a couple of mushrooms and tomatoes, half a jar of Branston pickle, curry powder and some rice. The result was Branston pickle curry. Other women said their finances had suffered when they divorced and became single parents.

Dolly mentioned how shopping wasn't an occupation or leisure activity as it is now. Lois also pointed to the gradual expansion in the culture of spending and, for very many Sixty Somethings, the really high-expenditure item was a house. Owner occupation was on the rise from the end of the war until at least the 1990s and, for Eleanor, getting on the housing ladder was considered very important even if it meant a 'fight' and 'hardship'. If you could achieve this, you would be okay. Many of the Sixty Somethings had both expected and managed to buy a house, although it was never easy, said Audrey: incomes weren't enough. Nonetheless, many acknowledged that it was simpler for them than for their children. Clara said she could buy herself a house at 24, but added that young people couldn't do that now. Alison said she'd managed to buy a nice house with five bedrooms when she was 33 or 34, adding that her daughter of the same age has a two-bedroom garden flat. Lissa had bought a house with a partner on a joint mortgage and, by the time they had split up, it had been very easy for her to get a mortgage on her own.

The women acknowledged how they had benefited from the housing boom. 'Without doing very much, you could move up very easily,' said Julia. She'd sold her flat for three times what it cost, and had then done the same again. Sylvie pointed out that there had been plenty of houses to do up and many Sixty Somethings had taken advantage of this. Winifred had renovated two derelict houses from scratch to get to where she is now, living in a single room with babies in the early days while the rest of a house was being restored. However difficult their journey, most women spoke of a positive destination. Olive was not alone in saying she had lived in a house she would never have believed she would live in. It was all about getting on to the housing ladder in the first place.

Social mobility

Mike Savage wrote interestingly in 'Changing Social Class Identities in Post-War Britain: Perspectives from Mass-Observation', published in *Sociological Research Online* in May 2007, comparing what people said in 1948 and 1990. Drawing on data from Mass Observation exercises, he found that people rarely self-ascribed a 'clear and unambiguous class identity and wanted to announce their identities in altogether more coded ways'. Although they were all most likely to call themselves middle class, their descriptions were tempered by a feeling that 'one does not talk about class' in the earlier period, and by a wish 'to mark their mobility and individuality' in the latter.

Nuanced accounts of social class and social mobility were indeed provided by the Sixty Somethings asked to describe themselves in these terms. Katherine for one pointed to the difficulties that arise in trying to pigeonhole people. On her own part, her origins were very much working class, but her jobs have been defined in both working-class and middle-class terms. She said that when she was a social worker there were more people in the job from working-class than middle-class backgrounds, and when she was a therapist there were more people from middle-class backgrounds because only they could afford the training. She had never been comfortable being labelled as middle class and thought retirement was brilliant because 'I can just go back to what I am'.

Others too questioned definitions of social class, with Geraldine expressing the common belief that there had been more changes between parental and grandparental generations than between her and her parents' generation. Violet echoed this view, suggesting that class was now thought of in a different way, with the upper classes less revered. She too saw the change occurring in her generation, with a greater emphasis on what could be achieved rather than the class you were born into. For Dolly it seemed that the rules had broken down. Money had taken over in importance. People could now work their way up and class, status and money had become intermingled. Tabitha offered a further insight, recalling discussing social class with a boyfriend in her twenties. He had said that the difference between working and middle classes is that the working-class person says, 'Have I got enough money for tonight?' while the middle-class person says, 'Have I got enough money until the end of the week or the month?' She thought the drift of this was correct and suggested that 'everybody's middle class these days, aren't they?'

With these provisos in mind, did the Sixty Somethings see themselves as having been socially mobile over their lifetimes? Unlike their parents, they grew up at a time of increasing educational and training opportunities, the economy was booming, manufacturing was in decline but jobs were plentiful. Moreover, professional, managerial and technical jobs were on the increase. Many of the women had availed themselves of what was on offer.

Two thirds of the 67 women thought, on balance, that they were in a similar social class as their parents and, in most cases, what they might describe as middle class. For some this was a relatively easy conclusion to reach. Sylvie, for instance, said she was 'all middle class through and through', Verity and Violet both said they were born middle class and stayed middle class and Ruby said she had remained within the professional middle class. Dolly said she was middle class because that's how she was brought up, adding that she's described as 'the posh bird' at work because she speaks properly. Geraldine came from a family of university-educated people and never doubted she'd go to university, 'not for a moment', even though she'd not been a particularly good student at school. For Lynne it was about having the opportunities her mother had never had. 'Definitely,' she said, 'even just owning my own house ... having a car, being able to go anywhere ... a passport.'

A few Sixty Somethings recognised that they might have been downwardly mobile socially, although usually from a middle- or upper-middle-class family background to more lower-middle-class occupations and income. This might have reflected not having gone to university, or being less concerned than their parents about their status and more interested in having a lifestyle they found rewarding in other ways. Jokingly, Mary's husband suggested she might have gone down in the world to which she retorted that, yes, she might have been in slightly higher echelons of society if she'd chosen someone different!

Tweegy and Norah were among those to say there'd not been much social mobility over several generations of their families, but by contrast many women pointed to the considerable mobility shown by their parents. Others elaborated on the more subtle distinctions across generations. Jo and Lindyloo, for instance, considered themselves to have moved from a lower to a middle position within the middle class. Lois, by contrast, thought she'd experienced some drop in standards because she'd come from a privileged family. She told of elements of snobbery in the circles her parents moved in but said that when she became an independent single parent it was 'much more about dealing with realities rather than putting people in boxes'. Molly said that while neither parent came from a middle-class background, her father's job had put him into that bracket, albeit not very comfortably. What it did, however, was create people like her who are middle class. 'I am middle class but it's a class that's been created for me, rather than inherited,' she said. She thought she'd lived within that artificial class all her life.

Others drew different types of distinction. Alice thought she shared her parents' social status even if she didn't share all their values, whereas Annie said she had the same values but more opportunities and was better off. Katherine, who never liked the middle-class label, really regarded herself as consistently working class but in a position to enjoy the things that society has designated as middle class. For Stephanie it was a question of moving from 'posh but poor' when she was younger to 'posh but rich'. A few women, whatever their origins, preferred to label themselves as socially fluid, stressing how they had friends from a wide range of different backgrounds.

More than a dozen Sixty Somethings regarded themselves as socially mobile over their lifetimes. Generally, they saw themselves as moving into the middle classes, or upwards within the middle classes. Chenhalls thought she probably fell into this category as she came from a generation of farmers and was the first to go to university. She had more friends who were better educated than the friends she would have had without her opportunities, and had a husband in a professional occupation. Even just moving away from her home village had seemed important. Jenny described herself as coming from a very working-class background but marrying someone from the 'ruling class'.

A few of these socially mobile women added provisos. Hannah, for instance, didn't see herself as the same as others who are middle class, and Olive said she still relates to working-class culture. Eleanor, who had personally 'moved up', defined social class as to do with culture and daily life rather than income. Zena tended to agree. She felt her social mobility had come about through her education and the people she had met socially rather than through her job. Stella found the question of social mobility difficult as she thought that neither her parents nor she fell neatly within a category. Her husband was from a working-class background and she said, 'I've got the trappings of middle class, but I don't feel middle class.' She added that she felt conscious, even now, of not speaking in 'Received Pronunciation'.

The number of grammar schools peaked in 1964, and were attended at the time by some one in four of all pupils. It is widely suggested that the opportunities provided by these schools were responsible for increased social advancement for young people from working-class backgrounds, the like of which has not been seen before or since. This point is, however, contested. An influential study by A.H. Halsey and others, *Origins and Destinations: Family, Class, and Education in Modern Britain*, published in 1980, found few differences in the social class backgrounds of pupils in selective schools in 1964 and 40 years earlier. Other research tends to suggest that while those who did make it to grammar school were likely to have done well, others who did not get in fared worse than they might have done in a comprehensive system.

Regardless of the evidence, there was strong support from the Sixty Somethings for education as a prime driver of advancement in their generation. Grammar schools, the education they provided, the expansion in university provision, and university grants were all hailed as enabling young people to move away from their social origins. Many women knew people who had benefited in this way. Sometimes it was themselves. Passing the eleven-plus was what Theresa thought made the difference for her, and Zena agreed. 'If I hadn't passed my eleven-plus, I would have been a lady in the flats [housewife in council housing]. That would have been my parents' aspiration,' she said. It was university and university grants that were important for Lynne and Olive. Sometimes the social advancement had been shown by others. Ruby, for example, could think of a 'significant' number of people from working-class backgrounds, where the father might have been a butcher or a steelworker, who became well-off middle-class professionals. Some women did nonetheless stress that not everyone was able to take advantage of these opportunities. Poppy was among those to point out that 'so many bright kids' did not benefit, Sarah adding that there was poor provision for those who did not gain places in grammar schools. Violet also wasn't so sure that grammar schools had aided social mobility and Minnie, while aware that lots of people in her generation said they were the first in her generation to go to university, felt there had been even greater opportunities in the previous generation. Certainly, a considerable number of the Sixty Somethings had parents, usually fathers, who had shown marked increases in social status. As Melissa pointed out, the middle class was expanding at the time, whereas it is at a more stable level now.

Whatever social status the Sixty Somethings achieved during their adult years was carried on into the autumn of their lives, when many reassessed and redefined how they spent their time. Their activities and reflections in this last stage of their lives are presented in the following chapter.

6

When I'm Sixty-Four...

The Sixty Somethings were in their sixties or early seventies when they talked about their lives so far, frequently comparing themselves to their parents. They hadn't lived through a war, they were more likely to have worked and had careers than their mothers, their standard of living was usually higher, they'd had the advantages of a good diet and a good health service and they believed they looked and behaved 'younger'. Perhaps most importantly, though, and due to a strong upward trend in life expectancy over their lifetimes, most could look forward to a longer life. When the NHS was established in 1948, around the time they were born, the average life expectancy in England and Wales was 70 years for women. By 2014, however, surviving women aged 65 years were expected, on average, to live for a further 21 years. The Office for National Statistics estimates that, on average, people these days can expect to draw a pension for up to 24 years. This is perhaps half as long again as in the generation before.

Feeling good

Recent research confirms not only that people are living longer but also that today's 65-year-olds are healthier, more mentally agile and more independent than in the past. This calls for a new definition of old age, suggests a group of academics from the International Institute for Applied Systems Analysis in Vienna. They argue in a 2015 article in *PLOS One* that it should be guided by how long people have left to live and begin only when this is fifteen years or less. On this basis, the post-war boom babies are still middle aged until they are 74, when they suddenly become old.

With the prospect of many years to go, most Sixty Somethings had given up paid employment and reached a point in their lives when they could, in principle at least, do exactly what they wanted. They were also a generally healthy group. Half said they were 'fighting fit', 'hale and hearty' or otherwise in good health with no significant condition, either past or present. Most of the rest mentioned issues that didn't affect them on a day-to-day basis, such as slightly raised cholesterol, taking blood pressure tablets or statins, a treated underactive thyroid or having had (or being about to have) a hip or knee replacement. A few also listed past conditions, such as premature menopause or an early hysterectomy, breast cancer, back problems, surgical interventions and a nervous breakdown, that were now resolved. That left a small number with ongoing disorders including chronic kidney disease, cancer, inflammatory conditions, rheumatological conditions and allergies, as well as problems with eyesight and hearing. Aches and pains seemed common across the board, but these were taken as a given.

In addition, the Sixty Somethings overwhelmingly described their current financial situation as 'comfortable'. As Stephanie remarked, house prices were a key factor in disparities in wealth within her generation. Home ownership doubled from around a third to two-thirds of households between 1970 and the mid-1980s, the period when many of these women entered the housing market, and soaring house prices since the 1970s, and again since the 1990s, had had a major impact on their putative wealth. Most of the women were homeowners and had money tied up in property. This did not necessarily make them feel well-off. Those like Jenny and her friends, who had few extra sources of income, could still feel 'skint' and describe themselves as 'the classic asset-rich cash-poor lot'. Having a realisable asset nonetheless placed them in a relatively advantaged position among their age cohort as a whole. It still remains true that members of their age group from working-class origins are less likely than middle-class families to be homeowners.

State and workplace pensions were another important source of income and wealth that ensured a good standard of living for many of the Sixty Somethings. Their generation was the prime beneficiary of the massive increase in retired households, with official statistics showing how private pensions rose from only 45 per cent in 1977 to 80 per cent by 2016. Disposable income thus grew more rapidly in retired than in non-retired households over this period and also led to an increasing income gap between those reliant on a state pension and those with an additional private pension. This was despite the doubling in value of the state pension in real terms over this period. For these various reasons, as widely pointed out, pensioners are better off than ever before even if, at the same time, there are enormous inequalities and an increasing number who live in absolute poverty.

Most women acknowledged their good fortune and, even if they didn't describe themselves as privileged (see later), agreed with Rachel and Robin about how much better off they were than when they had started out. Meg said it was hugely ironic that at a time when she was earning less than ever, she was almost entirely debt-free. She had accessed her private pension and been able to pay off the mortgage. Those without occupational pensions, not surprisingly, could find their finances more stretched. Jenny, for instance, talked about all the 'lefties' she knew who'd expected to be 'nuked' and didn't have decent pensions. She said they had all lived for the moment.

Other sources of income for the Sixty Somethings were husbands who were still working, property and investments, money-making activities and inheritance. Primrose had suddenly become better off on the death of her elderly mother. Several women also suggested they had benefited from being shrewd with their money. Miranda was brought up to pay off debt, Melissa said she didn't waste money and Verity said she would ring round to get £30 off her house insurance. She also rarely threw clothes away.

Overall, the women's finances were sufficiently good for a considerable number of them to be giving financial help to their own children, often contributing to a deposit for a house. They were part of the 'Bank of Mum and Dad' that, according to the Legal & General, lent more than £6.5 billion to their children for house purchase in 2017. A Social Mobility Commission report in March 2017 on the impact of family support on home ownership among the young pointed out how this meant that over one third of first-time buyers received financial help from their families. Some women said they felt they weren't being greedy if they could give something to their children, one saying she was reluctant to spend money because she wanted her children to have it. Not everyone took this view though, and there were some mothers who didn't see giving everything to their children as part of their parental role.

Nor did all women have money to spare. Katherine, for instance, had gone full circle 'from bedsit to bedsit'. She'd looked at her pension when she'd retired and thought she'd better take in two lodgers. So she was now back to using her sitting room as a bedsit. Flavia, who was reliant economically on her husband, said she would like to retire, but 'I wouldn't really have enough to live on independently the way I'm going at the moment ... He saves, I spend.' Ruby was comfortably off but didn't have sufficient resources to be able to move back to London as she would have liked. A few said their financial situation had been adversely affected by divorce.

With time, health and money generally on their side, the women were busily engaged in a wide range of activities. Nobody sounded as if they were sitting around not doing much. Whatever they were doing, they wanted to keep active and keep alert. 'There's no way we're giving up,' said Verity. Many subscribed to the 'use it or lose it' philosophy, Meg talking about the importance of mental stimuli to keep the cognitive functions going and Lindyloo about doing lots of puzzles to keep her head together. Tabitha listed all the oversubscribed educational activities for older people in her area. 'We've got the money, we've got the leisure and we've got the inquiring mind,' she explained.

A sense of purpose was apparent in the way the Sixty Somethings spent their time. According to Beth, it was to do with self-improvement, being intellectually active, feeling stimulated. Lissa talked about the importance of having a focus for every day, particularly if you have worked all your life and have a strong work ethic. 'I have to do something constructive every day,' she said, maybe gardening in the morning in order to allow herself to 'lollop' around in the afternoon. 'I must always have a quid pro quo for myself.' It's when she has a long breakfast, enjoying herself reading the paper and doing Codeword, that she feels old.

Mary made a similar comment. She said she absolutely loves reading and, even though she is retired, 'I still think I'm young and ought to be doing things, I feel guilty if I decide to just sit down and have a read.' She thought many of her peers felt under similar pressure and asked themselves if they should 'be exercising, or doing something for somebody else, or doing something useful?' For her, reading was something she was allowed to do on holiday. 'But am I on holiday now I'm retired? I don't know,' she wondered. Melissa too was anxious about not having things to do to make her leave the house. 'I'm fine if I've made myself a list of things I've got to achieve. But if I haven't done that, I can potter around in my dressing gown and waste time and then I feel bad at the end of the day.'

So many of the women stressed how they were different from their parents at their age, and how their expectations were higher. According to Chenhalls, 'we're much more demanding – not thinking that after three score years and ten we should pop our clogs.' She thought that her generation had far fewer preconceptions of what was and was not suitable for them to be doing. Eleanor said her life was completely different from someone her age even 30 or 40 years earlier. 'I can't believe how quickly that's changed. I feel that I'm like my mother at 50 rather than at going on for 70.'

A change of direction

According to Department for Work and Pensions statistics, the numbers of over-65s still working more than doubled in the twenty years between 1995 and 2015. Nonetheless, although some Sixty Somethings remained in work, most had 'retired' from their previous main employment. A few were in part-time occupations or engaged in self-employed or creative activities where the concept of retirement was somewhat different. Perhaps surprisingly, coming to the end of their careers and leaving a full-time or long-term job was often a boost to their morale. It hadn't made them feel older but had given them a new lease of life. 'People used to think they were old when they retired. Now life starts again at that point when there is time to do all sorts of things,' said Robin. 'Time to do new things, volunteer, do something completely different, meet new people,' added Carol. Nonetheless, not all had plans to retire. For example, Clara wanted to keep on working 'because I want to stay young and work keeps you young', Miranda hoped, as a musician, to just carry on playing and doing bits of work for ever, and Julia planned to keep going as long as she could.

There were also ten women among the 67 where retirement and pensionable age had different connotations. These were the WASPI women affected by recent legislative change and so called because of the Women Against State Pension Inequality campaign set up in their name. Retiring from paid employment has traditionally been linked with reaching state pension age. For all women born before April 1950 this was at 60 years, even though it was at 65 years for men. The 1995 Pension Act sought to equalise this age for men and women and set out a timetable to achieve this, through gradual steps, by March 2020. The 2011 Pension Act, however, accelerated this timetable to bring in equality by the end of 2018. It also determined that the state pension age for both men and women would increase to 66 for anyone born from October 1954 onwards. These unanticipated changes impacted on women born during the 1950s who, with very little notice, found themselves expected to work for longer than they'd planned. Of these WASPI women, four had fully retired, two were winding down and about to reduce their hours, three were working part-time and one was working full-time.

Everybody had an individual story to tell about why they had retired when they had. Eligibility for pensions was key for several and, for Bella, meant she'd left work when she was 63 years, 11 months and 25 days old. Three were offered voluntary redundancy and took this as an opportunity to retire. Others retired because they weren't enjoying the job, were unwell or feeling under undue stress, or thought they were past their best. Sometimes office structures were changing and the women no longer felt they fitted in. Yet others retired to look after sick partners or other family members, or because they had ideas of other things they would like to do.

Overall, and in retrospect, there was a lot of enthusiasm for retirement. Elizabeth, however, thought it was a 'class or economic thing'. It was alright if you had money. And this was the case for most of the Sixty Somethings who felt they were 'comfortably' off. It is perhaps worth noting that the word 'comfortable' was used both by women with decidedly modest means and women who might be described as wealthy.

Winifred echoed others when she said: 'I think retirement is brilliant. I absolutely love waking up in the morning and feeling that the time is mine rather than belonging to someone else ... Although I liked my job, I hated being in someone else's employ. I always hated that. So I find that an absolute joy ... I just keep waking up and thinking today I can read or write or garden. That's pretty much it really.' And Frances said, 'Love it. I'm happier now than I've ever been in my life. Unequivocally. There have been wonderful times in my life ... I loved having my babies, small children, loved all that ... I'm most at ease now and absolutely engaged in what I'm doing. I love it.' She added that she is thankful every day that she doesn't have to go and teach 30 kids in a classroom. Not having to get up in the morning and live against the clock, not having tasks you absolutely have to do, and looking forward to activities without being too old and decrepit to enjoy them, were some of the aspects appreciated by the women.

There were of course provisos. Lindyloo would recommend retirement 'so long as you were prepared to accept that you might not be able to do everything that you wanted to do'. In her view there were no real disadvantages except financial ones, a point reiterated by several of the other women. Barbara missed being part of a team, and Meg thought that retirement meant she had lost her purpose. She felt her identity had been tied up in her job. As she said, 'Once that's not there, you really need to have a structure about what replaces it. I'm working on that.' There were a handful of women who had been apprehensive about leaving a lifetime of work and found it took time to settle in to their new life. Sarah thought that if she had her time again, she would plan it better. Chenhalls couldn't see many disadvantages of retirement, although she'd had to be 'dragged kicking and screaming into it'. Not surprisingly the WASPI women were among those who could see retirement negatively, albeit for a very different reason. Hannah, for instance, said she won't get her teacher's pension until she is 66 and that is 'six years of pension that I've been robbed of ... I can't think of anything else you buy into and then they say we're not going to give you what you've bought. We're going to give you half of that.' Carol said she was in the most disadvantaged year group and felt that the financial advantage she had hoped to enjoy was 'now being stripped away'.

Keeping busy

Giving up formal work was a significant turning point for many of the Sixty Somethings, even if the term 'retirement' was something of a misnomer. Although they may have given up their main occupation, many took on other commitments and responsibilities, both paid and unpaid. Some were working freelance in their fields of expertise, and many did voluntary work. For example, Betty had retired early but then worked at the Citizens Advice Bureau for 20 years, Helen had taken on part-time work as the secretary to the trustees of a private school and Julia was working three days a week as a visitor experience host at the Museum of London. Lilian, who had retired on her sixtieth birthday, was elected as a Labour councillor one year later. Both Lissa and Persia had trained to become magistrates. Almost all Tabitha's friends had voluntary occupations of one kind or another and she herself was a prison visitor. Robin was involved in voluntary community activities in the places she lived in both England and France. There was a rich variety of other voluntary activities, such as animal welfare, the environment and home visiting. For Frances, looking after her mother 'ticks the voluntary work box'. One woman suggested the country would fall apart if it wasn't for volunteers of her age.

Some women not doing any voluntary work at the time were thinking about the possibility, particularly if it fitted in with their special interests. Lois wasn't in a rush as she didn't want to commit to anything she didn't really want to do, and Alison said it was important to choose your voluntary work carefully because some roles are very boring. Several women were wary of being tied to a regular activity and thereby losing their newly earned freedom.

Retirement also provided an opportunity to spend time doing what they really enjoyed. Frances, for example, was working on her art full-time and successfully exhibiting her work, Molly was selling her silk paintings and Miranda was fully involved with her music. Winifred and several others were concentrating on writing. A few had business interests. Sylvie regarded herself as a self-employed landlady, renting out rooms and a flat. Chenhalls had a couple of properties she managed, and Jacca ran a bed and breakfast. The Sixty Somethings also mentioned reading, joining book and film clubs, learning foreign languages, going on courses of different kinds, visiting museums and galleries, playing golf and a host of other things.

Travel was another priority for many of the Sixty Somethings. Carol was among those to say that retirement brings expectations of travel, although for some women, such as Lois, 'holidays are about people not places for me'. She preferred to go and visit her daughter in Scotland. Jane also had little desire for adventurous holidays. 'I've done everything I wanted to do – go abroad, hitch-hike in Greece, sleep on beaches … What a misery that was in a way. But I've done it and I don't want to do it again … It was horrible actually, but it was quite good fun. I thought I'd get in tune with nature.' Charlotte too avoided travel more than she might, in her case because 'I struggle with booking flights online and stuff like that'.

Many of the women had visited places they hadn't seen before, taken city breaks, been on Pilates or yoga holidays, gone on cruises or been sailing, hired villas for the whole family, been on walking trips, and so on. Mexico, Sri Lanka, Australia, New Zealand, Corsica, Greece, Romania, Italy, India, Bhutan, Turkey, Peru, Canada and the Galapagos Islands were among the specific destinations mentioned. Many women weren't as adventurous as when they were younger and preferred organised holidays and comfort, but some still were. Clara, for instance, was about to make a trip to Mongolia with a friend. They would have a driver and stay in people's homes with no hot water and Asian-style loos. 'That's an adventure,' she said. She worked to pay to get herself to the furthest corners of the planet and planned to get to the Antarctic before she died. Dolly wasn't going so far afield but had started doing 'younger' things on holiday breaks. She'd recently jumped out of a tree on a zip wire and been able to show her sons a photo of herself in a wetsuit. She liked being able to surprise her children.

Camper vans evoke memories of the 1960s and 1970s, and it was noteworthy that several of the Sixty Somethings had one. Bella thought hers would be used more and more as she probably 'won't want to do so much sitting round in airports' as she gets older. Elizabeth said hers was bought with pension money and was 'a godsend'. Jo said she didn't go on foreign holidays but liked going away in the camper van to 'walk and talk and drink and read'. Primrose had recently bought hers and was looking forward to using it more. Ruby had recently bought a caravan for breaks away.

In addition to all these activities, many women had new or expanded roles and commitments. Grandparenting was pre-eminent. Well over half of the 67 had grandchildren, mainly biological, and almost all played some part in their care, whether on a regular or irregular basis. Indeed, it has been suggested that the UK economy would grind to a halt if grandparents went on strike. Charities Age UK and Grandparents Plus estimated that grandparents were worth over £7 billion to the economy in 2013, a figure almost double that of 2004. The high cost of formal childcare and the increase in families where both parents work have meant that grandparents are called on to play an ever-greater role. In a series on retirement for the *Guardian* in 2017, Amelia Harris presented evidence to suggest that around four in five grandmothers of a child under 16 in England provide some form of childcare, some also reducing their own income by giving up work sooner than they might otherwise have done, or working fewer hours.

The Sixty Somethings nonetheless raised questions about what should be expected of them as grandparents. While they loved their grandchildren, there was an issue about the commitment they were willing to make. They talked about an expectation that they would be there to help. Most were happy to act as a safety net, but providing care on a regular basis was another matter. Alison said her daughter had told her she might love her grandson so much that she'd want to look after him more than a day a week. She'd had to say she did love him very much but didn't want to look after him more than she already did because 'I do have a life'. Eleanor also said she wasn't the sort of grandmother who couldn't wait to get her hands on grandchildren, adding, 'I love them to bits, but I have my own life.' She always says yes with goodwill if she can babysit, but doesn't want to be tied down. Tweegy mentioned friends who had retired with plans to do all sorts of things, and maybe earn a bit of money, but found all their time went on grandparenting duties. Lilian, who had only just given up work, was resistant to making a regular commitment until she had worked out how she wanted to spend her retirement.

Other women were, however, very happy to make a commitment. Some had regular duties, such as Annie, who took her two grandchildren to school in the morning and fetched them in the afternoon every Monday and Friday. This worked well and was 'lovely for everyone'. Betty and her husband looked after their granddaughter on Mondays and Wednesdays and were both very keen on this role. Robin spent one to two days per week with her enlarged family, going out for meals, cooking and eating at home. Entertaining the children was 'an enormous part of our job'. She would do more walking and cycling with them but they were currently too small. Barbara had resisted a regular carer role but changed her mind once she had seen her new grandson. She was now looking after him one day a week and loving it. Jan stopped her counselling work to help with her first grandchild.

Frequent but not regular help was another approach to grandparenting. Jo, for instance, was very happy to look after grandchildren but not on a routine basis. Olive looked after her grandson about once a week, but only when his mother had something she wanted to do, such as go out for a run. If grandparents lived at a distance from their grandchildren, they might go and stay with them for a week or so at a time.

Many Sixty Somethings were still hoping to become grandparents before too long as they were 'cracking on a bit'. Charlotte, who was still working full-time, said, 'If one of my children asked me to help with one of my grandchildren, that would be a bigger priority than carrying on working.' Friends had told her she should be thinking of herself now, but she'd insisted she would enjoy looking after grandchildren. Not everyone fully agreed. Although she thought her grandchildren absolutely gorgeous, and she loved them to bits, Jenny did admit that looking after them could be 'very boring' and that 'I clock-watch'.

The Sixty Somethings have been called the 'sandwich generation' because they may be looking after not only grandchildren but also elderly parents. Due to increased life expectancy over recent decades, more have surviving parents than ever before. Indeed, and according to the Office for National Statistics, there were almost fifteen thousand centenarians in the UK in 2017, an increase of over 85 per cent from 2002. At the latter date there were also almost 600,000 people aged 90 years or over. More women than men fell within these categories. One implication, according to Age UK, is that one in three of the UK's informal carers are at least 65 years old themselves. And those over 75 years and in this role have increased by a third since 2001.

Many women had surviving parents but were divided between those with and without care responsibilities. Even parents of a considerable age could still be reasonably independent and it was then a case of keeping an eye on them rather than providing more direct care. Eleanor's mother was 85 and looking after herself but she has 'something linked up so I know if she hasn't boiled the kettle for several hours'. Persia's 94-year-old mother lived independently a short walk away but they spoke on the phone every day, saw each other most days and went to the supermarket and on holiday together. Tabitha had been one of her 95-year-old mother's carers for the past 15 years.

Katie went through various stages. She persuaded her parents to move into a small modern house over the road from her own when she realised they were no longer coping in their large old house. This solution worked for a few years but as dementia, sight and hearing problems worsened, their problems multiplied and she recruited her brother to help move them into a nearby care home.

Elderly parents could bring their stresses, particularly if they were demanding and difficult and mother and daughter had never got on especially well. One woman told how her 92-year-old mother complained that she wasn't supporting her enough although 'she looks perfectly good to me'. Sometimes women seemed trapped into looking after parents who didn't want to go into a home, or felt guilty visiting elderly relatives in care homes. On the other hand, elderly parents could also cause worry when they didn't want any help.

A few of the women also had, or had had, responsibilities for looking after a husband or partner. Sometimes this was during an illness, and sometimes when they had a chronic condition or were disabled in some way. A few women said they had retired from work because of a partner's ill health.

An additional family responsibility affecting Sixty Somethings was the presence of so-called 'boomerang' children. The Office for National Statistics reports that 3.4 million young people aged between 20 and 34, a million more than ten years earlier, were still living with their parents in 2017. These figures represented about one in three young men in this age group and about one in five young women. Research is divided on the advantages and disadvantages for parents. One body of opinion suggests that having adult children around can be disruptive to recently retired parents hoping to embark on the next stage of their lives, but another points to an acceptance of 'family projects' that help and support children while they progress to adult independence, particularly in middle-class households.

Six women mentioned boomerang children, with young people sometimes returning home for more than one spell. Living with parents was often seen as a way to help adult children save, or to give them somewhere to live until they could find a sufficiently well-paid job. There was no evidence of any stigma attached to returning home, and no parent voiced particular concern at having their children back with them. Some mothers were indeed keen for their children to know there would always be a room for them should they need it.

Staying fit

As well as looking after others, the Sixty Somethings were busy looking after themselves. Was it important to them how they looked and what did they do to keep themselves healthy?

Looking and behaving as young as possible is widely celebrated and the media have certainly caught on. Channel 4's *Ten Years Younger* is a good example. This offers (usually) a woman a makeover that could include cosmetic surgery and cosmetic dentistry, as well as a new hairstyle and make-up, and asks 100 members of the public to judge her age before and after. A success is hailed if the woman is seen as at least ten years younger by the end. Three books accompany the series and offer tips for those not lucky enough to take part in the programme. In the print media, magazines such as *Saga* regularly feature people who achieve beyond what might be expected for their age, and the *Financial Times* has run at least three series on how older people are redefining later life. There seems to be a feeling that anyone not giving up when they reach three score and ten is a cause for celebration. Maye Musk, who says she's 'just getting started' as a model at 69, is a good example.

The majority of the Sixty Somethings were concerned about their appearance, and just as much as ever. Indeed, Charlotte was shocked and surprised that the older she gets, the more bothered she is about how she looks. 'We don't want to look old-fashioned, or dated,' said Carol. The women were also at pains to stress how different they were from the generations before. Although many of their mothers and grandmothers may have paid as much or more attention to their appearance, their dress code was more likely to reflect their age. Barbara suggested that she and her peers wear things, like jeans, that their mothers would never have dreamed of wearing, and Bella said her mother had discovered Crimplene in her sixties. 'We're the purple hat brigade,' she added by way of contrast. There were exceptions, of course. Hannah described her parents as 'raging against old age' and said her father, and probably her mother too, would wear all sorts of exotic clothes. And Deirdre described how her mother had been to Paris in her eighties and come back with a white Fender leather jacket and tight silver leather trousers. She wore them with stilettos.

The current generation in their sixties and seventies liked clothes and tended to dress well. Tabitha said the grandparents picking children up from school are all smartly turned out. Their style, however, tended to be 'relaxed' and their choice of garments no longer defined their age. Several women said they went shopping with their daughters and bought the same kind of things from the same shops. Jeans and jumpers seemed to be a staple, although 'interesting' clothes were also favoured. Audrey, for instance, said she liked clothes that were unusual without being crazy. Nobody wanted to look like mutton dressed as lamb although, as some women pointed out, that concept was very outdated. Some lamented how jackets and high heels had only very occasional outings from the wardrobe.

The purpose of dress had also seen a shift. Margaret said that until she was well into adulthood, she'd thought how you looked to the other sex really mattered. The importance of individual style had now taken over. The Sixty Somethings wanted to shock with fashion in their younger days, said Beth, and the legacy is wearing whatever you like. Mary said 'we are much more likely to dress for ourselves', and for Charlotte this included making an effort without it being obvious. Another important change in their generation was that, as Patricia said, 'we just carry on the way we have been doing'. The Sixty Somethings' lives were not bound by their age in the way their parents' before them had been.

There was a strong divide among the women when it came to their hair, and again they were not following any strict convention. Many said they'd had much the same hairstyle for years, whereas others said they'd chosen shorter styles as they'd got older. Skelton said she'd come round full circle to the hairstyle she'd had as a teenager. Whatever their current style, it was probably the one they were going to stick with. Margaret's usual refrain at the hairdresser was 'same again … sensible little bob'.

Whether to colour or not to colour was an important question for most women. The first and largest group comprised those adamant they never wanted to go grey and who, like Sylvie, began dyeing their hair at the first sign of a change in colour. Lissa, for example, would carry on dyeing her hair 'so long as I can lift my arms to do it'. Second were those who had dyed their hair for a while but had now stopped. Rachel said, 'I just feel I want to accept who I am and how old I am.' Theresa had stopped dyeing her hair when she was about 60 as she's 'not bothered' about it. Third, there were those still colouring their hair but wondering whether or not to continue. Hannah was among those building up the courage to stop. Fourth, there were those yet to go grey. Flavia fell within this group but had started to think about what she would do if her hair lost its natural colour. She thought she was too mean to start paying to dye it, but realised she might change her mind. And fifth, there were those preferring to remain 'au naturel'. These included Audrey, who said she never worried about her appearance, as well as Winifred. Looks did matter to her, but her hair had gone a nice whitey blonde and she liked it.

Make-up similarly divided the women. Patricia wouldn't be seen without it, and Elizabeth hadn't been out of the house without mascara since she was about 11 'and that won't change'. Tabitha said 'I'm an absolute make-up fiend', and Beth would almost never not wear eye make-up even if she knows she's going to be on her own all day. Annie always wears eyeliner and pointed out how 'most things become a part of you'. On the other hand, there were women who used little or no make-up. Mary, for instance, said she has 'more or less ditched it. I'm confident enough just to not bother with it', and Theresa said much the same, adding, 'but I would not dream of going out without having my toenails painted.' Although make-up wasn't of interest to some women, there was also peer pressure against wearing it in some circles. Jacca said she had friends getting frantic about their ageing looks, but others were more natural. In her view, 'they'd always been into authenticity, so why not now?' She'd persuaded lots of people to stop dyeing their hair, she said.

Wrinkles are an unavoidable part of growing older and were generally accepted by the Sixty Somethings, who drew attention to their own. Mary thought lived-in faces were very intriguing and Frances concurred, suggesting they reflect 'how you're feeling inside'. 'I like the laugh lines,' said Beth, and 'no way would I get rid of my wrinkles,' added Molly, who said she smiled a lot. Dolly also thought she'd earned her wrinkles: 'they're badges of honour.' 'I've got sodding wrinkles. It doesn't matter,' concluded Jacca.

The idea of cosmetic surgery was usually frowned upon even if the outcome might be welcomed. But women were pragmatic. Dolly talked about bags under her eyes that it would be fantastic to get rid of but said, 'I know what can go wrong and fortunately I've found someone who thinks my bags don't matter.' Jude said she might look in the mirror and think she could look better with a facelift but wouldn't be prepared to have any unnecessary surgery, while Patricia said she knew several people who might consider 'nips and tucks around the face' – if they could afford it. Liza also might have liked a facelift but doubted she'd ever get round to it. For Sarah, having surgery would be like 'crossing a line'. She said she'd love to look better than she does, but to do anything about it would be really self-indulgent. Even Bella, as an 'old hippy', said she'd quite like to get rid of her jowls, although she clearly had no intention of doing so.

According to Alison's hairdresser, many more women have nips and tucks than one might imagine. However, of the Sixty Somethings, only one said she'd had cosmetic surgery. In her case it had been a facelift for 'terrible bags under the eyes'. It was not to make her look 30, she said, but to make her not look 80. 'It was actually to make me look my age. People asked if my mother and I were sisters. She loved it but, as you can imagine, I wasn't so keen.' This is not to say that other women had not had procedures to enhance their appearance. Pedicures, manicures, tinted eyebrows and eyelashes, shaped eyebrows, whitened teeth, facials, facial electrolysis, and laser treatment to remove a facial blemish were all mentioned. As one woman said, 'I have time and disposable income.'

Looking after oneself is bound up with lifestyle. Katherine said that if she was going to live another thirty years, she would look after her body like some people look after a vintage car. According to Elizabeth, Sixty Somethings 'have to think about healthy living while older generations just led a healthy lifestyle'. The women seemed in agreement that their generation makes a much more conscious effort to exercise, that it is more organised. Their parents got exercise, but through the walking and other physical activities in their daily lives.

The Sixty Somethings, almost without exception, extolled the virtues of taking exercise and keeping fit and gave the impression they do what they can. Many belonged to gyms which, Poppy said, are 'absolutely full of older people'. This is unsurprising in the light of a 2016 report on the most frequent users of the 77 gyms in the UK run by Nuffield Health. It emerged that 60- to 69-year-olds visited an average of seven times a month as compared with 20- to 29-year-olds, who visited an average of five times and, moreover, that the average age of their most frequent gym user was 67 years old. How often the Sixty Somethings actually went to gyms was unclear. Charlotte, for one, found that belonging to a gym was helpful even if she didn't go. She knew she could if she wanted to. Sarah pointed out that belonging to a gym provided a bit of insurance.

The women provided a long list of other things they did to keep healthy. This included swimming, walking, cycling, tennis, yoga, Pilates, Zumba, gardening, carrying grandchildren, climbing stairs rather than taking the lift, gym equipment at home and walking the dog. Liza went around the country jive dancing and said she's now got the best figure she's had for years. Lissa said she and her friends are all very focused on keeping themselves going.

The importance of diet was also mentioned by most women, who said they were careful about what they ate. Watching their weight seemed a priority, but keeping healthy was important too. Some pointed out that it wasn't always easy. Ruby, for instance, thought her generation was concerned about diet but that eating habits are very strongly entrenched and can be difficult to change. Her downfall was a sweet tooth. Old habits could be helpful too. Sylvie said her generation grew up knowing about cooking and that junk food and takeaways didn't come naturally to them. Even if we have no money we know how to make soup, she said.

Wine was the most significant blot on the otherwise fairly healthy lifestyles of the Sixty Somethings. Very few still smoked, even if they had in the past, and only one said she still occasionally used recreational drugs. But drinking wine, and to a lesser degree often other forms of alcohol, was commonly mentioned, often accompanied by some expression of guilt. Many said they drink more than they should, Carol admitting that her consumption was 'never quite within government guidelines' even though she bears them in mind. 'Last night I didn't even have a glass of wine,' said Clara, 'which is quite a miracle.' In Ruby's view, a lot of people her age have got used to large, and quite dangerous, quantities of alcohol on a daily basis.

Excessive drinking, and a rise in alcohol-related deaths, among older people has been widely publicised. The Office for National Statistics has shown that 55 years and over is the only age group showing a rise in alcohol-specific death rates between 2001 and 2016, with younger groups showing a decrease. Moreover, rates among the over-55s have risen faster among women than men over this period. Many women acknowledged the dangers and had consciously cut down on their alcohol consumption. Quite a few had decided to drink only at weekends, or only on certain days of the week. Persia's rule was that she would only drink alcohol in social situations and never on her own. Betty also didn't drink at home but would take a bottle if she went out. It was, she said, a social lubricant. Nonetheless, the women were able to justify some level of drinking. Sarah had once been on an alcohol-free diet that had been too miserable to carry on with, while Chenhalls pointed to the difficulty with conflicting advice on healthy living. Her strategy was to pick on things she found appealing, one of which was to have a glass of red wine a day.

'Love is love and not fade away'

There is a conventional wisdom that younger people don't like thinking about their parents having sex. The reality, however, is that many older people either have active sex lives or wish that they did. This was confirmed by David Lee who, writing in *Archives of Sexual Behavior* in 2016, reported on 70- and 80-year-olds from the English Longitudinal Study of Ageing. Almost one in three of the women over 70 were sexually active and of these about a third said they had had sex at least twice in the past month.

The Sixty Somethings had a variety of relationships and arrangements. About half were married and living with their husbands, ten were cohabiting with partners and five had non-live-in partners. The rest were either widowed or single and living alone. Some relationships were long-standing, while others were more recent, and although women on their own could be 'happily' or 'gleefully' single, they could also be open to finding a new partner. As part of the Sixties and Seventies generation, they weren't worried about being 'conventional'. Clara thought if you can find someone you want to be sexually active with, go for it, 'why not?', although she was not willing to share her 'front door with anyone again'. As mentioned in the previous chapter, Molly and her partner of 20 years had lived in the same building for the last three years and only cohabited at weekends.

The women were not asked directly about their sex lives, but many told their stories. It was clear that sex was often still on the agenda. This came out both when women specifically talked about their current sexual relationship, either with their husband or a partner, and when they said they missed sex.

Both married and single women fell into the latter category. Two married women, for instance, said their sex lives were reduced to near zero, one saying it was a 'source of some misery' and the other hoping it was a temporary situation. 'Sex' was also mentioned by a number of women as something they used to do but didn't do any longer. 'A bit more sex than I've been getting in recent years' would be nice, intimated Melissa, a sentiment echoed by Audrey, Barbara, Miranda and Stephanie. It was something they all missed. Hayley concurred, saying, 'Sex, but I don't know if I could be bothered now. I'd have to shave my legs.' She added that 'the only reason I'm not having sex is because nobody's offered. It's not because I've given it up or because I think I'm too old or anything daft like that.'

Not all women missed sex though. One married woman with a current sexual relationship said she didn't mind about it one way or the other. While still having sexual feelings, she found it 'a great relief not to have to express them too much'. And not all those without current partners wanted anybody new in their lives. Quite a few had got used to living on their own. Maureen, for instance, said, 'I don't want another relationship. Too much hassle.'

Dating sites have become widely available for all age groups and there is evidence that the ease of finding sexual partners is leading to an increase in sexually transmitted diseases in older age, with rates having doubled among 50- to 90-year-olds over the past decade. The Sixty Somethings knew people who'd used these sites even if they hadn't themselves, and there seemed little stigma or embarrassment attached to them. At least two, and probably more, of the women had found partners via the Internet. Sylvie was amusing on the subject, having been a recent convert. She had gone on Tinder and met two much younger men. The second, a man in his forties, had become her current lover. While she thinks women her age are terrific, she says she can't stand older men. She thinks they are so reactionary.

Other women had thought about using dating sites and might in the future should they be single and wanting another partner. Melissa was going to have a go, while Persia and Lindyloo said 'never say never' and 'I might'. Others were not against the sites in principle but thought it unlikely they would use them. They said they were not motivated enough, had got very used to being on their own or weren't sure they would want another relationship if anything happened to their current partner. Beth said, 'Maybe I should bite the bullet and see what happens ... I would quite like to feel that I was special. But ...' She thought that if she was going to give dating sites a try, she should do it before she was seventy. Others were not so sure. Miranda didn't want to try a dating site and Alice said, 'I couldn't. No, I just couldn't.'

So how old is old?

The Beatles wrote and sang 'When I'm Sixty-Four' back in 1967, when they were feeling young. The song spoke of a vision of getting old, with the man saying to the woman:

> You can knit a sweater by the fireside
> Sunday mornings go for a ride,
> Doing the garden, digging the weeds,
> Who could ask for more?

It was a cosy vision of life for the elderly 'ordinary' folk of that era, and clearly the young rock legends regarded being in your mid-sixties as being old. But what did the Sixty Somethings regard as old age? When did they think they were going to get there?

Their answers varied, with some suggesting an actual age and others responding in more general terms. This concurs with the different ways that physiologists and medics or statisticians and social scientists might refer to old age and the definition of older people. The former are more interested in the process of growing older and the onset of functional decline, while the latter necessarily rely on some type of categorisation. The Office for National Statistics, for example, commonly refers to those over 65 as 'older people' and those over 85 as the 'oldest old'. By contrast, the World Health Organisation has defined an 'older person' as someone 'whose age has passed the median life expectancy at birth'. According to the British Medical Association, this is currently 81.2 years for men and women combined in the UK.

The women who gave numerical answers most commonly said 80. 'When you hit 80 then it's curtains really,' said Melissa. Often it seemed that they chose an age far enough in the distance to not be too worrying. As Barbara explained, 'I used to think of it as 70, but now of course at 69 I don't. I think actually 85 to 90.' For Chenhalls it was 'always ten years older than you are'. Norah admitted that 'I'm not sure when I get to 90 that it'll still be 20 years older than I am'.

There seemed a definite reluctance on the part of the Sixty Somethings to define their own age group as 'old'. They seemed to choose to say 90 or older if they knew somebody of that age who was still going strong. Frances said that 'even my mother doesn't seem old to me'. She was 92. Miranda's mother was still 'amazing' at 93 and still teaching Norwegian. Zena said she'd say 90 because she could think of two women of that age who go swimming and are really good role models. Lindyloo agreed that 'at the moment it's probably 90 ... but when I get to 80 I'll tell you.'

There was widespread agreement that not everyone ages at the same rate, and many of the women preferred to describe the characteristics of old age. 'When you feel diminishment of activity,' said Jan. 'When you can't drive and you're dependent on others,' said Clara, adding that 'old is when your body seizes up and your eyes and your memory have gone fut, and you're not looking forward to each day.' 'It depends how well you are, physically and mentally,' suggested Violet and several others, while Tweegy said it might be related to when someone goes into a home or needs serious care. In Alison's view age is not the most important thing: 'It's your attitude, that's what makes you old,' she said. This seemed to be in Bella's mind when she said old was when her mother 'hit the Crimplene' in her sixties and stopped being the flamboyant creature she knew as a child.

Not surprisingly, given what they said, most of the Sixty Somethings didn't want to feel old themselves yet. Lissa said that 'if somebody described me as elderly, I'd be horrified', admitting nonetheless that she would have referred to her mother as elderly at the same age, and Zena said, 'I won't be old until I feel too old to do things.' But there was too an acknowledgement that they weren't as young as they once were. Minnie knew she would be referred to as a pensioner if something happened to her and she made front-page news even though 'I don't feel old and I don't even look particularly old'. Melissa, who had just had her seventieth birthday, kept 'telling myself I'm in the fourth age ... so yes, I am old ... even though I don't feel it', and Alison admitted to sometimes having to give herself a pep talk if there was somewhere she couldn't be bothered to go out to. 'I'm 66. I have said it. It's hard, but that's how old I am,' said Poppy.

Attitudes to growing older

Even if between 65 and 79 is the happiest age for adults, as suggested by the Office for National Statistics, growing older is inevitable. What did the Sixty Somethings feel about this prospect? Some women saw ageing in a positive light whilst others found the whole idea horrific. Many were somewhere in between, saying they were philosophical and accepting, but nonetheless worried about particular things that might happen to them.

Frances was 'very very positive. I look forward with great interest and I'm enjoying what I'm going through at the moment.' Jane said, 'I think it's very wonderful. I'm not the same as when I was younger. I found being young incredibly hard, dealing with jobs, dealing with relationships, having responsibilities … I think life should be a journey and by this stage one ought to feel incredibly happy and well. Which I do.' She had shed the major responsibilities of looking after ageing parents and running a business and it was a relief not to be constantly thinking "I should do this, I should do that". I would not wish to look younger, I would not wish to be younger … I am very very happy how I am.'

'I love it,' said Hayley. 'Whenever I don't like it and I start to ache, I think of all the people who died so young who'd give anything to swap places with me.' She says she writes silly songs and rude poems which are a bit bawdy and shocking and thinks it's a great compliment when people tell her 'I'll never look at my grandmother the same way again'. She's lost weight recently, proved to herself that she does have willpower after all and is having a better social life. In all, 'I quite like the person I am now.' Molly thought, 'I don't think we're afraid of getting old because we're still bobbing around in this cloud of optimism we've always had.'

At the other extreme were Eleanor ('It stinks'), Elizabeth ('I hate it'), Helen ('I don't like it') and Norah ('I'm absolutely dreading it and terrified'). Jan and Liza thought it was scary and Tabitha felt 'in many ways ageing is absolutely pants. Growing old is not fun. I always say to people you spend less on clothes as you get older, which is just as well as you have to spend it all on your teeth and your eyes. But apart from that it's quite liberating,' she added. 'If I wanted to lie in bed all day, or eat chocolate all day I could, or watch television all day … Nobody's going to say "What are you doing?"' Jenny could also see both points of view: 'It oscillates between oh my God, I loathe it, to absolutely enjoying every second and being as positive as hell.'

The majority of the Sixty Somethings expressed less extreme views. They realised they had to accept the ageing process and tried to make the best of things. Sarah, for instance, said, 'I'm trying to learn to love it, but I am rather fearful', while Jo's approach was 'just total pragmatism and fingers crossed'. Stella was stoical. For some the solution was to try not to think about it too much, or to resist it. Clara, Hannah and Melissa said they were 'in denial' and Chenhalls said she was almost ashamed to be getting older. Alison said she and her friends try to turn it into a joke by saying things like, 'My ankle's really hurting, I must be getting old.' Sylvie's attitude was just to say she's 43 and a half if anybody asked.

Most women had things they were looking forward to. Many of these were associated with being retired, in good health and reasonably well off. They included spending more time with a partner, doing things with family, having grandchildren and getting to know them, being master of their own time, new projects of different kinds, working a bit less, more travel and holidays and fresh challenges, as well as more specific things such as a daughter's wedding or a particular trip. Verity was looking forward to doing more with women friends. They'd already talked about 'sharing a house and employing young men to look after us'.

There were, unsurprisingly, also particular things that women commonly disliked or worried about. Aches and pains, feeling more apprehensive and anxious about minor matters and forgetting things were mentioned. Also being reminded of your age, such as when you have to show your older person's pass or a well-meaning stranger offering a seat on the train, were day-to-day events that riled. In the longer-term, becoming unwell themselves, a partner or other family member getting ill, developing Alzheimer's or dementia, losing people they loved, needing to be cared for and becoming a burden, becoming a carer for a loved one, being badly treated in a care home, and maybe not living to see their grandchildren grow up, were real concerns. Several stressed that it was all downhill from now onwards. Was it still worth planting a new tree, wondered Jacca?

Growing old disgracefully?

Many Sixty Somethings could quote at least the start of 'Warning', Jenny Joseph's poem about getting old. It begins:

> When I am an old woman I shall wear purple
> With a red hat which doesn't go, and doesn't suit me.

There is a hint of the disgraceful, which increases as the poem goes on:

> I shall sit down on the pavement when I'm tired
> And gobble up samples in shops and press alarm bells
> And run my stick along the public railings
> And make up for the sobriety of my youth.

As the poem nears the end, however, it becomes clear that the narrative is but the dream of somebody still expected to pay the rent and 'set a good example for the children'. It is the reverie of someone hoping that one day, when they become old, they will be able to shock a little and start to wear purple.

Did the women remember the poem because it struck a chord? It seemed it often did, although not for Jo, who called it a 'fucking cliché'. But, nonetheless, did the Sixty Somethings plan to grow old gracefully, disgracefully or gracelessly?

Most decided on gracefully, even if they included a caveat. 'Gracefully – I don't like people who make an exhibition of themselves,' said Tabitha, who was echoed by Verity who commented, 'Gracefully, I think. I don't want to grow old disgracefully. How embarrassing is that?' Alice too didn't want to embarrass her children but wanted to do 'gracefully' in her own way: 'I don't want to do anything because it's assumed it's the way it's done,' she said. Bella and Helen also decided on gracefully, the first because she hadn't got the energy for disgrace, and the second because she'd already been there and done that.

A bit of disgrace was, however, called for by many of the women. Lilian opted for 'gracefully sliding into disgracefully', and Elizabeth said she would aim for gracefully, although 'I'm likely to drop the odd swear word to surprise people'. Katherine thought she was growing old very gracefully according to her standards, but acknowledged that some people might not agree: 'I flirt with young men because it's totally okay now. Mind you, I'd probably die on the spot if anyone took it seriously'. Some went even further. 'Disgracefully. Easy peasy,' said Hayley, and 'life's too much fun to be a grown up,' added Molly. Sylvie said she would be utterly disgraceful and planned to carry on doing what she's doing and enjoying herself. Some of the women liked to surprise or even embarrass their families. They didn't want to be thought of as the predictable older generation. Liza and her partner's skit for Comic Relief, in which she dressed as a 'naughty nun' with a corset and whip, provided a good illustration. Others experimented with their appearance, Lynne mentioning that she still has pink bits in her hair.

It was apparent that many of the women liked the idea of being disgraceful even if they weren't sure it was for them. 'I guess the right answer is disgracefully,' said Skelton, 'it sounds a bit more interesting. But I'm going to go for gracefully.' And Jan said, 'I'd love to grow old disgracefully, but I'm not sure what my family would say about that.' Lois thought there was a risk that growing up gracefully makes one invisible. 'So I think the disgracefully one is quite appealing … I don't think it's me particularly but I'm all for other people doing that,' she said. Tweegy thought the same: 'Oh I think disgracefully. One wants to have a bit of fun … I don't mean I'm going to suddenly start taking drugs … [but I'll] wear what I want … [and] if I want to spend money on an expensive holiday I will … But I'll still meekly go along to church.'

There were only a few advocates for gracelessly. Audrey made this choice because 'I don't care. I don't think I'm a particularly badly behaved person to be honest. I don't think I'm disgraceful. I think I'm graceless and just rolling with it really.' And Norah said, 'Gracelessly … I think I'm too proper to be disgraceful, and … graceful, I have visions of twinsets and pearls, and beautifully coiffed hair. Well, I'll never achieve that.' Ruby thought she would like to grow old gracefully but expected that gracelessly was more likely: 'I think that's the nature of ageing – graceless. Grumpier and needier and not able to look after yourself.' Sarah made a similar point: 'Gracelessly is a very difficult one … I hope I don't do that … but I probably will.'

Some people didn't go for any of the three choices on offer. Olive planned to grow old 'decently', Betty 'happily, contentedly', and both Hazel Grace and Theresa decided on eccentrically. According to the latter, 'I want to be a little bit dipsy, a little bit peculiar, I'd like to be more someone people would think, "my goodness, what's she doing? What's she wearing? Why's she saying that?" rather than "Granny's sitting in a chair being quiet".' Several women said they just wanted to be themselves.

Jude compared herself with her parents, suggesting her generation are more spontaneous. They had accepted there were certain things they wouldn't do as they got older, whereas her generation thinks that just because they're older doesn't mean they don't want to go out and make a fool of themselves or roar with laughter. Her life had always been a reaction against their lack of spontaneity.

Some people were still paid-up members of their generation, said Geraldine, and others agreed that not much changed as they got older. Part of the legacy, suggested Jenny, was that no woman she knew took anything sitting down. 'We all challenge everything in quite an anarchic way,' she said. According to Molly, they'd got to the point where they didn't really care, they'd do what they wanted anyway. It was liberating for many. Katherine, for example, had made dramatic changes in her life and, since retirement, embarked on becoming a Buddhist nun. From being 'a very clean and neat hippy' who always liked clothes, hair and jewellery, she had shaven her head and started wearing very different clothes. The things she used to be passionate about, such as theatre, concerts and art galleries, seemed to have disappeared into the ether and now nothing is more important to her than sitting on her cushion and racing around helping people.

The final chapter

The Sixty Somethings could be said to be in the autumn of their lives and might yet have the winter to come. A record number of people have reached the age of 100 in the UK in recent years, the number increasing fourfold over even the past two decades. In 2015, there were 14,370 centenarians and 850 people reaching 105. Since the early 1980s, life expectancy had increased by an average of nine and a half weeks a year for females. These differences do not, however, apply to everyone in this generation. Where people live makes a difference, with marked inequalities in well-being and support between the most and least deprived areas of the country.

Even if they were active and well, most Sixty Somethings had given some thought to the future, and there were few without worries. The deaths of family members, friends and acquaintances had brought the reality home. The general attitude seemed to be that they were not going to live for ever, but they were going to make the most of the time they had left.

Remaining healthy was a priority, and the possibility of developing dementia, or some other serious illness, particularly if there was a family history of the condition, was a real concern. One woman, for instance, said there was bowel cancer on her father's side of the family and dementia on her mother's side and she did worry. She was not alone, many women saying they'd become increasingly fearful as they'd got older. Lynne's biggest fear was that she reached a point where an illness, probably a mental illness, meant she was locked in. 'The thought of being locked in is the worst thing ever,' she said. Women also worried about a partner becoming ill as well as the possible need for them to become a carer.

Being patronised as they got older was something else the women dreaded. Many had seen how others had been treated and didn't want it for themselves. Olive told a story of a professor in her seventies who went to hospital for an operation on her leg. When asked what she would be doing at the weekend, she'd retorted by saying she would be speaking at the United Nations. How would they be treated if they became dependent? Katherine for one had told her younger friends to please keep an eye on her if she had to go into a care home. For many, however, that was a last resort. Hazel Grace was adamant on this point: 'I'm never going in a home. I'm going to kill myself,' she said. She'd seen the 'good' but horrible home her mother had been in and thought there could be nothing worse.

On the other hand, the women didn't want to be a burden on their children, even if they worried who might look after them if they didn't have families. This was a concern for Persia, who was currently giving her own mother a lot of support and wondered who might do the same for her. Ruby also worried about the consequences of having no children of her own. As discussed in the previous chapter, Jacca found it scary at times having no children to ring and check on her, as she had done with her mother for 20 years. Winifred too was worrying about who might give her a bit of help when she found it too difficult living in her house on a steep hill. She didn't know if she could find a companion to live in with her.

Some Sixty Somethings had taken active steps to prepare for the coming years and the time when they would be less able to do things for themselves. Several mentioned writing living wills or setting up a lasting power of attorney, and there was a concern that money didn't run out. Others were busy decluttering, or thinking about it, and otherwise sorting out their affairs. Hannah said her husband kept talking about funerals and saying they should organise theirs. Alice said she would quite like to plan her own.

Indeed, many women specifically said they didn't want to live for ever and some were more worried about living too long than about dying. Charlotte said, 'I don't want to live until I'm 90, but knowing my luck I would.' It was fine if she was physically and mentally healthy, but otherwise she didn't want to be kept alive. 'It's very low where I want to step off,' she said. 'I don't need to be high non-functioning. I absolutely don't want that.'

She was not alone. Many women voiced their approval for euthanasia in the right circumstances and several had links to Dignitas or Dignity in Dying. Some were hopeful that the law on assisted dying might have changed by the time they might want to avail themselves of it. Lindyloo said it was important to her to have the choice when it came to her own death, and to be able to make it as positive as possible both for herself and others that cared for her. Clara wanted to be able to look after herself to the very end without a carer or going into a home. 'If I become a major burden I want to be allowed to remove myself from the planet. Without anyone being prosecuted for helping me. I don't want to become a burden. And I won't. Legally or illegally, I won't.' Lynne said she was prepared to go to Switzerland to end her life if it came to it, and Primrose did too. She would do it herself otherwise, she said. She'd had lots of dogs so knew ways of doing things. For Tabitha, who was intent on being independent but also pro-euthanasia, it was the uncertainty of knowing when she would die that fazed her. If she could find a way to organise something, she would.

Despite their thoughts on the future, and a recognition that they were not going to live for ever, most Sixty Somethings nonetheless remained optimistic and were going to make the most of the time they had left. Without doubt they had led interesting lives, and were continuing to do so. Yes, they were getting 'old', but so what?

7

How's It All Turned Out?

Sixty or so years after the Sixty Somethings were born, the world has moved on. These women and their generation have achieved their own, sometimes notorious, status. Many so-called Baby Boomers began life in relatively frugal conditions, grew up to take advantage of the booming economy and growth in welfare provision, benefited from a good education, led a fairly free and easy existence in adolescence and early adulthood and thought they could change the world. Reality set in to some extent during their adult years, when most had raised families and secured work that gave them status and money. Often they were able to get onto the housing ladder and profit from the increased value of property over their lifetimes. By now many have retired into the next busy stage of their life, pursuing their own interests and projects, volunteering and travelling, and looking after grandchildren. Some people say they are privileged, but they are more likely to say they were lucky. And, as they repeatedly pointed out, the Sixty Somethings were themselves luckier than an awful lot of others in their generation.

Has the world changed?

There is little doubt that Britain today is a very different place to the Britain the Sixty Somethings experienced in their younger days. Had things turned out as they'd expected, and what impact did they think they themselves had actually had?

At a personal level, and almost without exception, the women felt they had been very fortunate. Often current circumstances far exceeded their expectations. Jacca, for instance, said she hadn't started out wanting a house, mortgage and washing machine and hadn't wanted to look as if she had emerged from the OXO advert. But she had grabbed opportunities over the years and had ended up with four houses, four cars and six washing machines. Hayley too had long surpassed her early ambition to have 'coloured sheets and hot water when you turn on the tap'. According to Jane, 'we all now lead lives that were once restricted to the wealthy elite.'

Sometimes the women were indeed somewhat surprised at their own good fortune and even perhaps a little guilty. 'I kind of feel a bit sheepish,' said Ruby, describing an ex-colleague in her thirties and her husband who have to work 'all hours'. She felt she'd had more disposable income than them both at their age and now. Being fortunate was made more problematic by the philosophy women had espoused throughout their lives. Alice found it difficult to square the 'age of protest' Baby Boomers with the current-day image of selfish Baby Boomers with expensive houses and massive pensions. Rachel too confessed to feeling guilty. Her present-day circumstances were 'not down to what I did' but it was still a 'difficult position to find oneself in'. Barbara reiterated how their 'luck' was not their 'fault', particularly 'those of us who did everything we could to argue for a fairer society'.

At a societal level, the question of change and impact is more complex. The V&A exhibition in 2016 entitled 'You Say You Want a Revolution?' celebrated 1966 to 1970 and addressed this issue. Polly Toynbee's review in the *Guardian*, which included her discussion with the co-curator Geoffrey Marsh, concluded that nothing was ever the same again despite the failure of most protest, the early death or tax exile of the great musicians of the day, and 'unglamorous, unhip Harold Wilson with pipe, Gannex and compromises' emerging as 'the unlikely sixties hero'. There were, nonetheless, important social reforms, the birth of the Open University and the 'extraordinary flourishing of high-minded collective endeavour' leading to a growth in voluntary and charitable activity with a wide range of community targets. On the other hand, Toynbee writes, there was also the growth of neoliberalism and anti-establishment individualism.

These points were iterated by the Sixty Somethings, whether or not they felt they'd played any direct role in the changes that had occurred. Their feelings were, however, mixed. There had definitely been progress but there was also disappointment and concern that much they had fought for now seemed on the brink of being lost.

Many mentioned the significant social reforms during the sixties and seventies. The Labour government of 1960 had, for instance, introduced the Murder (Abolition of Death Penalty) Act 1965, which meant the last hanging took place in 1964. Capital punishment did remain legal for some other offences, such as espionage, treason and mutiny, for some years, but was never again carried out. Barbara said she'd been passionate about the issue in her teens and 'I felt something different had happened in society' when capital punishment was outlawed. The Divorce Reform Act 1969 was another significant piece of legislation that affected many women. In essence this made divorce more accessible and available with proof that a marriage had irretrievably broken down. The Abortion Act 1967, which legalised abortion by registered practitioners, was also important to the Sixty Somethings. These were reforms that had endured and were life-changing.

Moves towards greater gender equality had also affected the lives of the women. The positive impact was still being felt of the Equal Pay Act 1970 and the Sex Discrimination Act 1975, both of which had in part been brought about through campaigns, protests and the rise of feminism. Women had changed the way they were regarded for ever, and even paved the way for women to laugh and swear, suggested Verity. Women's liberation had of course also been massively encouraged by the availability of the Pill. Many women emphasised what a huge difference this had made to them. 'Sexual permissiveness … makes so much more sense,' said Alison. It was a 'good legacy we've left', being able to get contraception without embarrassment.

These and other social changes were important not simply in their spheres of influence but because they were linked to the mood of the time. There was a new sense of tolerance and Liza suggested the generation has been associated with a decline in discrimination. She gave the example of single mothers who'd been given a bad time in the past but were now accepted. Lissa agreed that her generation was responsible for widespread changes in attitudes, such as towards gay people, people outside London and regional accents, and Violet mentioned more openness about mental health. Many women attested to the greater fluidity today, in social class, in the nature of families, in sexuality, that had stemmed from the sixties and seventies, with much emphasis on the acceptance of varieties of sexual orientation. This had been a massive change, established with the Sexual Offences Act 1967, which decriminalised sexual acts in private between men aged at least 21 years in England and Wales. Homophobia hadn't gone away completely, said Julia, but it was no longer regarded as deviant by most people. It was certainly talked about more and, according to Tweegy, sometimes too much. She gave the example of an author heralded as gay, saying, 'I'm not really interested in what he does in bed. If he writes a good book, I'll read it.'

Alongside greater tolerance of individual choice came greater recognition and intolerance of abusive behaviours of all kinds. Changing attitudes to child abuse provide an example. Lois suggested that 'when we were young there was a really prevalent view that men can't help it ... the idea that girls get sexually assaulted ... men can't help it and therefore some of these things are going to happen.' Nowadays, she said, behaviours that might once have been regarded as a bit of a joke in families would not be tolerated. An influential article by Nigel Parton in the *British Journal of Social Work* in 1979 charted the journey to a greater recognition of the problem of child abuse in Britain. The catalyst was almost certainly the case of Maria Colwell, who died at the hands of her stepfather in 1973. Due to the wide coverage by the press, and the intervention of key politicians and organised groups, the case resulted in a public enquiry and subsequent legislation.

Greater freedom to be individual took other forms too. Dress codes became less formal and decreasingly tied to age, and people began to wear what they liked. As mentioned in the previous chapter, the Sixty Somethings were likely to go shopping with their daughters and buy similar clothes from the same shops. Beth suggested a legacy of her generation is wearing what you like. Freedom of expression was another right gained during the sixties which again reflected the prevailing ideology. For example, the Theatres Act 1968 abolished censorship on the stage, and Mary Whitehouse, founder president of what became the National Viewers and Listeners Association, was less than effective in the mid-sixties in her attempt to halt the decline of British morals with her 'Clean Up TV' campaign.

Also, in 1960, Penguin Books were successful in overturning the charge of publishing obscene material, in the form of explicit sex and use of hitherto unpublishable language, in D.H. Lawrence's *Lady Chatterley's Lover*. The trial became symbolic, not just of shifting attitudes to sexual openness, but the way these had been caught up with issues of social class, exemplified by the prosecutor Mervyn Griffith-Jones's notorious question to the mixed-gender jury, drawn from a range of social classes: 'Is it a book you would even wish your wife or your servants to read?' Decades later his son told a journalist that this last remark was a rare act of improvisation and that, as soon as he said it, Griffith-Jones realised he had blown the trial. Rather than being banned, the book became a bestseller and one that most Sixty Somethings have almost certainly read.

Another enormous change witnessed by the Sixty Somethings has been the increase in the foreign-born population within the UK, from 1.6 million in 1951 to 4.9 million 50 years later. From the 1970s onwards, the proportion of those born in Europe went up through our membership of what has now become the European Union. Lissa was among those to say how much lives have changed over her lifetime, highlighting issues surrounding immigration and community cohesion. Difficulties facing those from black and minority ethnic backgrounds were convincingly shown by surveys conducted by Political and Economic Planning in the 1960s that demonstrated the discrimination they faced in employment and housing. The Race Relations Acts of 1968 and 1976 came shortly afterwards and made it illegal to 'refuse housing, employment, or public services to a person on the grounds of colour, race, ethnic or national origins'.

All Sixty Somethings benefited from modern technology, from labour-saving devices in the home to electronic devices. Sylvie talked about how it was 'brilliant' that domestic tasks had been made easier, while others focused on telecommunications. Norah referred to connectivity and how we can now talk instantly to each other across the globe. Lois contrasted the instant news of today with how things had been in the past. She recounted a story of someone who had been in the cinema when the Second World War broke out and had no idea what was happening until she got home and heard it on the radio.

Most Sixty Somethings had electronic devices, whether computers, tablets or smartphones, following the national trend. Smartphone ownership in the UK, for instance, has gone up dramatically in even the six years between 2012 and 2018. Statista statistics for this period demonstrate that, for 55- to 64-year-olds, a rise from 19 per cent to 51 per cent. The same data source indicated that 5 per cent of the 65+ age group owned smartphones in 2012 and 18 per cent in 2015. At the time of writing no comparable information was available for the subsequent years.

All the women were computer literate to the extent they felt they needed to be, and many were extremely competent. WhatsApp and similar programmes used to maintain regular contact with their families were popular, and many women contrasted the way they keep up with their children with the limited contact they'd had with their own parents when they were younger. There were, nonetheless, mixed views on social media. On the question of Facebook, some women used it on a regular basis while others were quite strongly averse to posting messages and pictures about their personal activities. More generally Elizabeth said, 'I think technology has made life better, definitely for me,' while Julia, Norah and Ruby were amongst those who could see both good and bad aspects, particularly the detrimental impact on younger people. Jane mentioned a report she'd seen that suggested the average person checked their mobile phone 224 times a day. 'I don't want to be like that,' she said.

Alongside the advances that had been made were expectations dashed. Few, if any, had anticipated the far-reaching effects of globalisation, neoliberal economic policies or banking crises. Maggie spoke for many in saying 'we thought we were moving forward but actually we don't seem to be'. Lynne was among those with great concerns about the state of the world: 'All the things we've done in my past life, as a Baby Boomer, all the opportunities, rights for women, women's ability to work, childcare ... All we fought for is just disappearing. I'm really worried about that. All those freedoms going. I don't understand,' she said. Margaret said she had been pretty optimistic but that now she was 'quite seriously upset'. Norah too thought 'it all seems to be going wrong'. She mentioned the song 'Age of Aquarius' from *Hair* and the film *Guess Who's Coming to Dinner* and said they'd summed up what she thought was going to happen. 'There would be peace and there wouldn't be racism,' she said. She'd seen the film again last year and had cried for 24 hours 'because I could remember how I'd felt when I first saw it'.

Current-day politics were also worrying. In her twenties, Lois had thought that society was becoming more left wing and more socialist. 'We were never going to have right-wing

Tory governments again – there's a joke,' she said. Patricia too found the swing from the left to the right 'sad and shameful', and Carol lamented what she saw as disappearing priorities of inclusion and looking after the weakest in society. Carol was of a similar view, saying that their narrative about making society more equal no longer seemed so desirable or possible.

Alison thought that 'politicians have got duller ... lost their gravitas' and spoke in soundbites. She says she shouts at whoever is being interviewed on the *Today* programme on BBC radio. Many Sixty Somethings lamented Brexit and Julia said she was very ashamed of the over-50s who voted for it. 'It's a much worse legacy than anything Baby Boomers have done in the past,' she said. It seemed, according to Meg, that 'some sort of horrible emasculation process has happened' since when her generation was younger. 'People would have been on the streets by now' protesting much more about Brexit and Trump than is the case these days.

In other ways too, the Sixty Somethings thought the progress they had made in their youth was being undone. Alice pointed to a backlash against feminism involving a move back to the extremes of femininity, saying there was no shortage of pink clothes and gendered toys these days. Beth too thought that some of the hard work of feminists, mainly in the 1980s, had come to little. She gave the example of people still doing PhDs on images of women in the media. 'I thought we'd dealt with all that,' she said. For Jenny it was that we were back to where we were 20 years ago, 'ready to be nuked'.

'We cast off personal restraint in the sixties, social restraint in the seventies, and economic restraint in the eighties,' is what a male university friend once told Meg. That may well be true, but how far were the Sixty Somethings and their generation actually responsible for any of these changes? It is a hard question to answer, and many of the women saw a variety of factors as important. There was a strong feeling that the war had made an enormous difference with a lasting impact. Men were coming home, women had been used to greater independence and responsibility than in earlier generations, austerity was coming to an end with an upturn in the economy, and there was a sense of freedom that seemed to be particularly instilled in the young. It was the previous generation and post-war investment that created the cradle-to-grave welfare that her generation benefited from, said Meg. They were only carrying on the work that had already been started. Many agreed that the Sixty Somethings were born into the mood and circumstances of the day and took things forward. 'I guess we took the baton and carried it on further,' said Minnie. There was a lack of deference and established institutions were challenged, said Olive, and with more and better education they were given extra confidence to campaign for change. 'We have been responsible for a shift in permissiveness,' thought Lynne, and 'I think we were responsible for lots of changes in attitudes,' said Lissa. 'A lot of good came out of the demonstrations that Baby Boomers led in their younger days,' added Liza. Julia thought her generation had started many things, such as the legalisation of homosexuality, that are taken for granted today.

The question of religion

The religious landscape in Britain has also been transformed over recent decades with, on the one hand, increasing secularisation among the indigenous population and, on the other, the emergence of new forms of religious faith as a consequence of globalisation and mass migration. Indeed, British Social Attitudes Survey data indicate that even between 1983 and 2014, based on responses to the question 'Which religion do you belong to, if any?', the Church of England population had nearly halved, non-Christian religious numbers had increased fivefold, and those indicating no religious affiliation had almost doubled. The Catholic population had remained steady, but this to some degree reflected the influx of Catholics from countries such as Poland. These changes are likely to have been even more stark over a longer time period. In line with these figures, church attendance has declined dramatically in all but the churches representing incoming population groups over recent decades.

Many of the Sixty Somethings had their own views on the declining significance of religion amongst people like themselves. Betty thought that economic reasons were important, with religion less needed in times of economic security. Persia stressed the role of education, suggesting that people had developed more enquiring minds and become more knowledgeable, and had therefore become more questioning about the meaning and value of religion. She felt that whereas families once went to church because they had always gone, individual members were now deciding for themselves whether or not they wanted to. Lilian added that this greater information enabled the questioning of more mythical aspects of religion. For Bella, such questions had been encouraged by the war. 'Where was God then?' many asked.

The growth of individualism, linked to education and the increased capacity for self-determination, further accelerated the move away from religion. As Lois pointed out, as people felt increasingly in control of their lives, they no longer needed a church or religion to define the meaning of their existence for them. Participating in organised religion also became much less expected. At one time, said Chenhalls, going to church was an important social occasion and you needed to go to be seen as respectable. Her point was reinforced by Sarah, who observed how most patients, when she'd been a nurse in the past, used to define themselves automatically as Church of England 'even if they didn't know what it meant'. 'They don't say it now,' she added.

While churchgoing became less common than in the past, religion continued to have a widespread function, albeit a changing one. Zena said that even though other settings now provided opportunities for social interaction, parents still wanted their children to be christened and to get married in church. Many also hoped they would attend church schools, for educational reasons, and accordingly needed to make obligatory appearances at church. Zena herself felt 'a bit of a hypocrite' when she had to get a 'signature from a priest to say I was a good Catholic' when applying to Catholic institutions for teacher training.

A weakening of morals was also linked to secularisation. Clara felt that a 'loosening of religion and more freedom seems to lead to less moral behaviour', whereas Helen suggested the causal link might be in the opposite direction in that the impact of two world wars on sexual permissiveness may have played a part. For Chenhalls it was about a mismatch between the church and modern times. She thought the church and its values, such as 'trying to stand up for the sanctity of marriage', were seen by many as out of touch. 'While it would have been seen as totally inappropriate for my mother's generation to say that, I think the following generation was prepared to say it,' she said.

Another view was that interests have changed over time. Sarah thought concern with 'spiritual matters' was on the increase, and Stephanie tended to agree. She felt secularisation was less to do with economics than about 'access to other forms of wisdom', citing the influence of the Beatles and the ideas they imported from India. 'John Lennon's "Imagine" was an anthem for all that,' she said. At the same time the Bible was seen as 'incomprehensible' and her generation didn't like the rigidity of the church and its 'rules'. She underlined the belief that young people wanted to be 'autonomous' and 'discover the truth for themselves'.

The Sixty Somethings' own religious pathways were in line with the changing times and fell into three distinct groups. There were those who had never been religious, either in childhood or adulthood, those who had been brought up within a faith but had abandoned it as they got older, and those who retained some religiosity throughout their lives, even if sometimes this was largely nominal.

Eleanor, Liza, Maggie, Margaret and Patricia were in the first category, mainly growing up with non-religious parents and not adopting a faith of their own. Beth was quite adamant about her lack of belief, saying that, 'Personally I have very little sympathy for organised religion – to the extent of being rather hostile. I love C of E churches but I do not love the religion that goes with it.'

Around a quarter of the women fell into the second category, brought up with some form of religion in their lives which they had since relinquished. Some such as Barbara, who had been a practising Catholic between the ages of 9 and 16 years, Chenhalls, who had been baptised into the Church of England, Primrose, who was brought up as a Christian, and Zena, who was brought up as a Roman Catholic, now described themselves as atheist. Lindyloo, whose mother had some Christian beliefs and who had gone to Sunday school as a child, also gave herself this label.

Many others called themselves agnostic or said they didn't have religion in their lives any more. Often it seemed it had just faded away. Zena, however, described her 'great escape' attributable to Pope John XXIII and one of the pronouncements of the ecumenical council which said that 'people should act according to their conscience'. As she said, 'that was my argument with my mother when I told her I wasn't going to Mass any more. Because it meant nothing to me and I'd be a hypocrite if I went.'

Despite the movement away from religion, the biggest group among the Sixty Somethings comprised those who still professed some religious faith, even if this was often with reservations. Alice, for instance, described herself as a Church of England Anglican. She was not a regular churchgoer but 'I hold to it, it's a significant element in life'. For Frances, Christianity was 'very important, in a doubtful and questioning way', while Jemima described herself as 'practising vaguely'. Melissa had been going to church for the past twenty years as 'it provides a space for me and I like the music'. Lissa and Sarah both said they were 'loosely' connected with the church, the former going to Evensong and ringing the church bells and the latter 'not really observant. I sort of care about it on a use it or lose it basis. I very occasionally go to Communion. It's a heritage feeling for me.' Skelton said that religion was 'not very relevant' to her. However, 'I do get comfort from it but I'm not an active churchgoer.' Tweegy said she was 'practising', adding, 'I'm not quite sure how much of it I believe, but I try.'

Some women, such as Norah, who called herself Christian and was 'currently at a Catholic church although not in full communion' had 'floated backwards and forwards'. Persia said she didn't go to church 'for years and years' but then had a car accident. 'Somebody came into the back of me. The car was a complete write-off. I didn't have a scratch. A motorcyclist helped me out of the car. I just looked at the car, and I didn't have a scratch. I just felt somebody was looking after me. And I went to church the next Sunday.'

There were others, too, who made considerable shifts in their religious faith. Flavia, for example, had been baptised at eight years in the Church of England and confirmed in the Presbyterian church when she was about 16. In her mid-twenties she had met the man, from an Orthodox Jewish background, who was to become her husband. She converted to marry him but doesn't practise Judaism 'in the least'. It was a step she later regretted and now thought that it's 'not a good idea to try to be someone you're not'. Katherine had also made large-scale changes in her beliefs and practices, moving from a Christian upbringing to becoming a Buddhist nun. Jacca said she had tried a few religions in her time, and Jan had made a somewhat pragmatic decision to become Church of England to meet her husband 'somewhere in the middle' between her as an Anglo-Saxon Protestant and him as a humanist who had been brought up as a strict Catholic. Mary, with a Church of England upbringing, now described herself as 'distinctly non-conformist'. She attends a Pentecostal church 'but you wouldn't know it was. It is essentially a group of Christians meeting together.' For her religion is 'not about stupid rituals but about love'.

Were the Sixty Somethings privileged?

Headlines in some British newspapers in November 2017, reporting on a politician's suggestion that selfish Baby Boomers are contributing to housing shortages by resisting the development of new homes in the countryside and antagonising 'avocado-eating millennials', are not alone in depicting those born in the post-war boom as privileged. David Willetts is among those to have written at length on the topic. His 2011 book, with the provocative title *The Pinch: How the Baby Boomers Took Their Children's Future – And Why They Should Give It Back*, outlines the thesis that the post-war generation, due to its large numbers, has configured the country to meet all its own housing, financial and healthcare needs. It points to the relatively disadvantaged position of the subsequent generation, who will have to work more for fewer rewards. Ed Howker and Shiv Malik had written on a similar theme the previous year in *Jilted Generation: How Britain Has Bankrupted Its Youth*.

Few would deny that there is a point to be made. There were an awful lot of people born in the post-war boom and longevity is increasing. The UK has an ageing population and official statistics show that 17 per cent of the population was over 65 in 2010, with that proportion projected to rise to 23 per cent by 2035. Women are particularly likely to survive into older old age. The need for health and care services among this group is likely to be high and not all will be able to provide financially for themselves. It can be argued that the next generation is at a disadvantage first, because they will have to contribute to the funding of healthcare for their parental generation, and second, because there may not be money left for them to inherit if their parents live into old age and spend their resources on their own care. The Resolution Foundation has estimated that those born between 1946 and 1966 are likely to gain around 20 per cent more in welfare support than they will have contributed to taxes over their lives.

The argument is clearly more complicated than this, and controversial at best. Some would argue, for instance, that the supposed selfishness and profligacy of the Baby Boomers has been used as a convenient scapegoat for the economic problems created by the policies of neoliberal politicians like David Willetts himself. The Sixty Somethings were asked what they thought on the matter. The vast majority agreed that they had been privileged, although not necessarily in the sense implied by much of the current-day rhetoric. Lucky was a term most of them would have preferred to use.

They agreed, though, that they had been privileged in the timing of their birth. Winifred saw her generation as privileged in that they hadn't had to live through the war, and Clara talked of privilege for women her age who were allowed to go out to work, earn a living, buy a house and feel liberated. Sarah added how her generation had benefited from missing out on many of the constraints facing both her parents' and her children's generation. For example, they had the Pill but missed AIDS. Moreover, they had the music. Patricia pointed to the free higher education they'd received, and how women could now retire when they wanted to, with good pensions. Lynne mentioned the benefits of the political enlightenment at the time she was growing up, the introduction of the National Health Service, career opportunities and the council-house building programme. She and Skelton were among those to tell how they had grown up in poor families whose fortunes had changed markedly for the better over their lifetimes.

But privileged in a wider sense was something the Sixty Somethings were more reluctant to accept. Rachel said she could understand why people might describe them as privileged, but it was not down to her generation, it just happened. They were beneficiaries of what the generation before them had fought for, and the post-world-war economy. Their lives had coincided with the growth in female employment, the birth of the welfare state and a rise in house prices. The country was booming and they were fortunate enough to have been born into a lucky era of history. As Jo said, 'I didn't create the housing boom and I'm certainly not taking any stick for it.' Meg also pointed out how the political ethos of the time, and politicians such as Beveridge, believed that it made economic sense to provide free education and health, and she thought 'how anyone can see that as privileged is bizarre'.

Moreover, their lives had not always been easy. While they had been lucky to have the opportunities presented to them, almost all the Sixty Somethings talked about the pressures and hardships they had gone through to achieve what they had. They had been fortunate but they had also worked hard. Many had suffered privations in their early years and had continued to 'make do and mend' into adulthood. For Jo and others, 'we struggled and saved and fixed things until we got to the situation we're in today. We earned every single thing we've got and I think we deserve it.' Lynne was of similar mind. 'We are perceived as getting more than our fair share now in terms of money that comes to us from pensions and because what young people don't realise – and what's forgotten by the press – is that we've paid all this money in,' she said. Others made similar points, with Olive saying that national insurance and income tax used to be called 'deferred wages' rather than benefits. In addition, and while the women had found jobs easily, they had endured sexual discrimination and harassment in the workplace, and had faced difficulties in a context of little or expensive childcare. Now, in their later years, there were still problems to be faced. Many were living on investments not yielding interest, and there was the prospect of finding and paying for care in the not too distant future amid forecasts of a substantial shortfall of carers. There was also the longer than anticipated wait for state pensions faced by the so-called WASPI women.

The Sixty Somethings were also anxious to stress that even if they had done well themselves, there were plenty of other people their age who hadn't. Enormous inequalities existed within their generation as well as between their generation and those before and after. They pointed out how only a minority went to grammar school, even when places were at their peak, and only one in ten went to university. Class had had a major impact throughout their lifetimes and not everybody had been equally fortunate. Beth commented that 'I think they're right to call us lucky, but I just think it's so difficult as it's different for different classes. There are still some living in terrible poverty – wearing the same clothes from one decade to the next.'

For all these reasons, there was a sense of indignation on the part of many Sixty Somethings about the way they were sometimes regarded by young people and the media. Lindyloo felt her generation should not be vilified for being fortunate, blaming the media for raising younger generations' expectations to an unrealistic level, while Liza thought her generation was being used as a whipping post. By no means all Sixty Somethings encountered young people who were critical of them. Charlotte said she didn't 'get a sense that the younger generation are feeling pissed off in any way', and Meg suggested that most younger people have pretty positive experiences of older people within their families, particularly given the greater role of grandparenting. Older people are largely invisible in many contexts, suggested some women, with Mary adding that the younger generation can be so wrapped up in their own lives and families that they don't really think about what their parents have been through.

Some Sixty Somethings were, however, on the receiving end of criticism, with their children blaming them for ruining their futures. Alison thought there was a tendency to put everything on the shoulders of old people and the last straw was when this included voting for Brexit. Of course, the children of Sixty Somethings who have done well may well be in receipt of good fortune themselves. The attitudes of some young people to her generation owning their own houses made Jo rage. 'It makes me so angry,' she said. 'It's so unfair and so misguided. They're all the people who're going to inherit all these bloody houses. They're such hypocrites.'

Generally, however, it was the media in its widest sense that most annoyed the Sixty Somethings. Although the *Daily Express* had launched a campaign for a Minister for the Elderly in May 2018 because 'the generation behind Britain's post-war prosperity is now neglected, exploited and even vilified', there was a feeling that older people were too often seen as a useful scapegoat and that the Sixty Somethings were depicted as overprivileged and ruining the life chances of younger people and, as Geraldine put it, effectively told to 'get off the planet and move over'. There was a view that such rhetoric was being unnecessarily stirred up. Jemima thought the images of older people 'using Botox and going on cruises' were inciting intergenerational discord, and that officialdom and the media could also be demeaning to older people. The road sign showing two bent old people walking with sticks was alluded to as a good example, as was an episode of *Montalbano* shown on British television in 2017 that depicted a 67-year-old prostitute who ended up murdered. Not only was the woman constantly referred to as a 70-year-old by the other characters, ageing her further and unnecessarily, but also anyone who availed themselves of her services was branded a gerontophile. But perhaps some things are on the move. Deirdre was certainly amused by a leaflet recently posted through her door advertising retirement apartments illustrated with happy, bouncy, hippy oldies. It was refreshingly different and, perhaps, not a bad selling point.

Baby Boomers?

The media are to a large extent behind the tendency to refer to Sixty Somethings as Baby Boomers, ostensibly to highlight the large numbers of them born in the post-war period. Live births peaked immediately after the war and again in the 1960s, but decreased in later years, possibly in part due to the impact of the Abortion Act 1967. Rates of births and deaths were similar in the late 1970s, after which time births have again exceeded deaths.

The term Baby Boomer first appeared in America in the early 1960s. It is clear, however, that it rapidly acquired connotations to do with lifestyle, attitudes and shared experiences, and that it has been used to imply more than simply a person born during a boom in births. This was acknowledged in 1983, when the 'Baby Boomer Edition', with its questions about rock music, television and films, became the second specialised version of Trivial Pursuit. Used in headlines such as 'Why Baby Boomers are hitting the bottle more than ever before', 'Baby Boomers are enjoying a second bite of the economic cherry' and 'Did we baby boomers bring about a revolution in the sixties or just usher in neoliberalism?', or in the title of David Willetts's book mentioned above, the term is undoubtedly intended to convey something about the identity of a generation even if the nature of that identity is not made fully explicit.

Asked about its meaning for them, a considerable number of the Sixty Somethings said the Baby Boomer label was a term invented in America, that it held no particular associations and that they had never before thought they might fall into the category themselves. Flavia said she didn't have a stereotype in her head and didn't think the general public did either. Many women were at pains to point out that there is nothing typical about being born soon after the end of the war and that people's lives are very different despite a similar age. Baby Boomers are not a uniform type of group, said Lois, while Geraldine thought she was quite different from some of her friends who had a less privileged upbringing. Zena described how her childhood was very dissimilar to her younger sister's, and also how she'd met a completely different cross-section of people when she'd gone away to university. Olive, Molly and Katherine also compared themselves with their sisters and their contrasting lifestyles.

For others there were distinct connotations of the label, which they may or may not have identified with. Audrey felt the term was largely negative and referred to a bit of a selfish generation that pulled the ladder up after them. She also thought it suggested living life in an autonomous way. 'This isn't the reality for many,' she added. Tabitha agreed there was a pejorative overtone to the label. 'We're just a rather unpleasant group of guzzlers,' she said. Yvonne Roberts suggested in a 2018 article in the *Guardian* that Baby Boomers may have attracted a negative press in part due to 'our irritating habit of hogging the cultural limelight, with constant references to the swinging 60s serenaded by endless revivals of Lazarus-like pop groups who refuse to die'. She also acknowledged that there may be some truth in the more serious charge of 'sabotaging our children's future, hoarding power and money while expecting those with the least to foot the potentially hefty bills as we march towards our nineties'.

Less negatively, some women linked the term Baby Boomer with being a teenager during the 1960s or participating in a sex, drugs and rock 'n' roll culture. For Beth, her sense of Baby Boomers was that they have an attitude towards public service and are perhaps not as materialistic as their children's generation. She also thought they didn't want to behave in the way expected of them. Rachel described the typical Baby Boomer as lucky, hippyish, anti-authority and ever youthful. This summed up many of her peers who were, though, only a section of the age group. A higher sense of their own worth, and more confident, was how Chenhalls described Baby Boomers, while Violet said they were people who have probably achieved financially. Fighting against the boredom of traditional earlier life, 'church on Sunday, liver and bacon on Wednesday', was suggested by Verity.

Once again the Sixty Somethings reiterated the variety of experiences of people in their generation. 'I don't think everyone was drooping around with flowers in their hair,' said Helen. Olive suggested that class made a big difference to life experiences and Julia agreed in comparing Baby Boomers living in London to those elsewhere. She thought the bigger group could be split into two, the liberal left and the conservative right, and that differences were partly attributable to where people lived. Katherine thought the term applied mainly to those who had moved away from home to go to university or teacher training college. Stephanie reinforced this point by describing the classic type of Baby Boomer as someone 'from the middle class and a southerner'. She said she had northern friends who were more or less bypassed by the hippy culture. This would not be true, however, of all the Sixty Somethings who had grown up, or gone to university or college, in this part of the country.

With all their provisos, not many Sixty Somethings readily claimed the Baby Boomer title. Some, fairly reluctantly, admitted they perhaps should as their teens had been during the sixties, because they considered themselves part of the sex, drugs and rock 'n' roll generation, or because they felt lucky compared to later generations. Others rejected the label outright. Bella saw herself as more Age of Aquarius, and Jacca said she felt more like a child or teenager of the sixties than a Baby Boomer. Others didn't identify themselves as Baby Boomers because they considered themselves too young or too old, or because they were definitely not representative of a sex, drugs and rock 'n' roll generation. In sum, it was probably the majority who were in fact bystanders to whatever it was they perceived as the Baby Boomer identity.

Was the generation really so different?

The Sixty Somethings, or Baby Boomers, may have gained a certain reputation and even notoriety, but how much do they really stand out as a generation apart? They were born at a distinct point in history, benefiting from the growing wealth of the country, the developing welfare state and greater opportunities in both education and employment. They were perhaps the first to have a distinct culture that was widely publicised, especially in relation to fashion, sexual mores, recreational drugs and, very importantly, music. And they were also well known for their 'alternative' ideas, lack of conformity, a wish to reform the world, a proclivity to protest and, now, a resistance to growing old. But how far were they really pioneers and how far were they simply opportunists?

Many of the women acknowledged the importance of opportunity in their lives. As they repeatedly pointed out, the war had been a landmark of enormous proportions. It had affected their parents' lives in a very direct sense, and it had made a difference to theirs as a consequence. In part this reflected the rebuilding of the country and its infrastructure, and in part parental reactions to the new environment. Even if there was no longer military action, there was now the threat imposed by the Cold War, and Eleanor remembered her mother telling her how facing the possibility of being blown up at any time during the 1960s meant 'there was a bit of the eat, drink and be merry because tomorrow we die'. The world was changing and the Sixty Something generation was in the right place to make its voice heard on the direction it should take. For those at university, provided with a period of relative freedom where issues such as earning a living were put on hold, there was the time to debate the social order and take any possible action on issues of social injustice.

Indeed, opportunity for some, although only a small minority of the generation, took the form of the chance to go to university or some other form of higher education. Generally, the Sixty Somethings, most of whom fell within this group, were encouraged in this ambition by parents who hoped they would have the opportunities they had foregone. Once away from home, many of the young Sixty Somethings took advantage of the possibilities presented to them. Often in a setting away from the parental eye, and in close proximity to many like-minded peers, they could behave as they chose, particularly in relation to the proverbial sex, drugs and rock 'n' roll. Opportunity was part of this picture in more ways than one. As Elizabeth for one said, she wasn't sure she'd have been 'sexually permissive or any of the other things' had she not gone away to university. And, on this score, even being away from home might not have had as much impact as it had on new sexual mores had there not been the Pill. This, as Minnie pointed out, wasn't invented by the Baby Boomer generation.

In many ways the young Sixty Somethings largely took forward the ideas and ideals of the previous generation. They had not started or stopped the war, they had not created the welfare state, they were not responsible for the expansion of higher education nor the production of effective contraception. However, they were in a position to move ahead in ways that they chose. As Meg described it, 'we were the first generation to do X, Y and Z because structures had been created to allow us to do it.'

But even given the accident of their birth, and the opportunities handed to them, were the Sixty Somethings so very different from their parents? Were the choices they made in marked contrast to those their parents made or would have made in similar circumstances? This is a difficult question to answer as of course the women have only their impressions of their mothers and fathers and may be oblivious to some of the things they did in their younger days. They were not present during the war, for instance, when it is likely that at least a few of their mothers did not behave entirely differently to the young women in *Yanks*, the 1979 film directed by John Schlesinger and starring Richard Gere. This depicts the commonplace affairs and liaisons between American GIs and English women during the war years.

Certainly the Sixty Somethings didn't invent hedonism. Pleasure seekers have existed from time immemorial, the term 'hedonism' deriving from the ancient Greeks and featuring in many religions and schools of philosophical thought. Hedonists, who might indulge in unconventional sexual behaviour, mind-altering substances spanning alcohol and drugs, or other 'unusual' practices, cross class boundaries and are depicted in both biography, such as the lives of the Bloomsbury Group, and fictional literature by authors too numerous to mention. They also form the subjects of all art forms from the past to the present. Baby Boomers were also not the first to favour communes and other alternative forms of living. This historical reality was widely recognised by the Sixty Somethings. Patricia, for instance, pointed out how talking to parents and the older generation confirmed that there was 'a lot more sex going on than was talked about'. And Eleanor spoke of her mother who, before her marriage, had been an actress in the theatre, where everyone smoked drugs and had 'liberal attitudes towards homosexuality'.

Most Sixty Somethings did still feel their lives were in sharp contrast to those of their parents, whose lives, in turn, had not resembled those of their own parents. However, this was not universally the case. Hannah, for example, said that her parents had lived 'very conventional working-class lives' but then went through a 'hippy phase'. She had felt rather the 'Saffy type', identifying with the sensible, straight-laced daughter Saffron, played by Julia Sawalha in the TV sitcom *Absolutely Fabulous*, in contrast to her outrageous mother and her friend, played by Jennifer Saunders and Joanna Lumley. She 'would have preferred they were more ordinary parents'. Hazel Grace had also come to feel 'more the Saffy' to her parents, who 'slept round massively', with her father having three or four mistresses at once. Liza and Deirdre both thought they had more adventurous parents than most people, but didn't say they'd felt embarrassed, and others too painted pictures of mothers and fathers who were not that different from themselves in their interests and activities. Meg also referred to her grandmother, who'd saved up her own money from 'the housekeeping' to send her daughter to university, as a role model. She'd been a strong feminist and Meg said, 'I would have loved to hug my grandmother and say "you were amazing".'

Many Sixty Somethings may, nonetheless, have come to more closely resemble their parents as they have grown older, even if they retained essential differences in attitudes and outlook. 'Some people had a wild period, but not for very long,' said Lissa. 'When you're young you can purport to all kinds of things, but when real life starts kicking in, then I think a lot of people swing back a little bit,' added Patricia. There seemed some agreement that as people got older and settled into partnerships and families and jobs, they could find they were more conformist than they'd realised. In Lissa's words, 'the responsible side took over from the irresponsible fairly early.'

Overall, then, it is probably fair to conclude that the Sixty Somethings have been both opportunists *and* pioneers. They had the raw materials given to them but, to the extent possible, crafted these into new forms of being. This applies to their attitudes towards ageing which, according to Robin, among others, have 'changed hugely'. Anticipating greater longevity than in previous generations, and with better health, older people are now confronted with the likelihood of many years on their hands after retirement. The lucky ones also have good pensions and can make real choices about their future lives. Indeed, the current attitude to ageing is strikingly ambiguous. Regular reports of ageism nestle uncomfortably alongside exhortations to youthfulness whatever your age. For this, however, there seems little guidance for, as Joanna Lumley lamented in the 2017 BBC2 programme *Absolutely Champers* with Jennifer Saunders, we don't really know how to look old these days. She said that in times past a woman her age would have gone grey and had a perm and looked like an old lady. Now people in her generation spend time wondering what to do with their hair. 'We try to look like how we've always looked,' she said. Certainly the overhead advertisement in the Underground in 2018 suggested that age is no reason to change behaviour. 'Keep your mum off Tinder,' it implored.

The Sixty Somethings and their legacy

Societies evolve and the circumstances and experiences of one generation are never the same for the next. There are, however, some stark differences between the lives of the Sixty Somethings and their children and grandchildren. 'Were we the last generation to be incredibly confident about being young?' asks Verity.

Whether or not that is true, there is more certainty that the privileged label attracted by the so-called Baby Boomers is unlikely to affix itself to younger generations. Most Sixty Somethings weren't so sure things would be better for their children, as they'd once expected. Home ownership is a case in point. The Resolution Foundation intergenerational commission report of 2018 has suggested that only half as many millennials (those born from round about 1980 to just into the twenty-first century) as Sixty Somethings own their own homes at the same age. Also, whereas it took three years to save for a deposit in the 1980s, it now takes an average of 19 years. This means, according to Yvonne Roberts writing at the time in the *Guardian*, that 'a third of millennials will, it is predicted, have a lifetime of renting with less space, poorer conditions, longer commutes and more insecurity than the baby boomers experienced.' So many Sixty Somethings pointed to the greater struggle their children were having with housing than they'd had, either saying they doubted they'd be able to afford their own home or saying they'd managed to buy something considerably inferior to what they'd achieved themselves. Eleanor said that her son had no chance of buying his own property in the foreseeable future, but he did have computers, a large television and a smartphone.

Employment and pay were also more problematic for younger generations. The Sixty Somethings had had no difficulty finding jobs, and jobs they wanted, but the situation had become very different. Elizabeth felt opportunities for bright post-16-year-olds were not there any longer, and nowadays people with degrees take two out of five non-graduate jobs, with a knock-on effect for the less qualified. One woman said neither of her daughters had got the jobs they wanted and were instead working on near-minimum wages. She said they take the attitude that 'something will come along'. Even when young people had gained good jobs, there was still a suggestion of lingering gender inequality. In Charlotte's case, the two males in her family earned more than the females, even if they had performed worse academically.

Jane also pointed out how stress levels could be raised these days, as 'now everyone knows they can possibly become a multi-millionaire'. She suggested that, in theory, there are no restrictions on social movement, upward mobility or income, and that that puts a huge pressure on people to work hard and do well and be seen to do well. Another problem, suggested Eleanor, was the 'obsession with getting every young person to university'. Expectations are raised, but then there aren't enough professional jobs to go around. Barbara added that young people are much more likely these days to see university as a meal ticket rather than somewhere to go to have their mind expanded. And that was Oxbridge she was talking about.

One thing the Sixty Somethings seemed agreed on was that their descendants were carrying on the trend towards greater inclusion and the creation of looser boundaries around gender, race and class. Audrey was among those endorsing the way young people, especially in London and other urban areas, have grown up in a multicultural world and enjoy friendships with people from all parts of the world. Minnie said how her generation had been careless about racial slurs in jokes but that younger people are more respectful. 'Kids will call me out. I've really had to learn to watch my language,' she said. Positive attitudes towards gender roles, among both males and females, were also commonly mentioned. Hazel Grace, for instance, said, 'I've created the right men for this new world,' and Beth, who described both daughters as good feminists, said, 'I know I've done my stuff there.' Many told of an openness about sexual orientation that had not existed when they had been young. This also related to talking about sex. Jemima related a story of an 11-year-old girl at school who said she'd got a boyfriend. He turned out to be 18 but, according to the girl, 'we're not having sex'. Three years later Jemima saw the girl pushing a buggy.

The popularity of marriage has dropped since around 1957, and the proportion of babies born outside wedlock has steadily increased since the 1960s. Currently, there are almost as many children born to unmarried as to married parents. This is an enormous change from the situation at the time the Sixty Somethings were becoming parents. Although it is too early to know fully about the circumstances of the millennials, there did seem to be a strong tendency for the children of the Sixty Somethings to be in favour of marriage, perhaps even more than their parents had been. However, the reasons for getting married were not the same as earlier, when some Sixty Somethings had wed for the sake of their families and appearances. Margaret said both her children were getting married, but not 'because they think it would be awful not to'. The impression from the women was that young people would have sex before marriage but, once they settled down, were likely to stay in monogamous relationships. Beth expressed surprise that her daughters would be horrified at idea of partners having affairs, and Maureen said her children had been aghast at stories of people sleeping around in the 1970s. Alice too thought her children's generation was more puritanical about monogamy with a spouse or partner and were shocked at infidelity. Violet said they'd been less disapproving of affairs in her day.

There was also something of the traditional in the way some members of the younger generation approached marriage. Lois thought there was currently a prevailing belief that the man should ask the woman, whereas her generation had often been more laissez-faire. Both Elizabeth's son and son-in-law had asked their prospective fathers-in-law for permission to marry their daughters before they proposed. She had been surprised and commented that when she'd told her father she was getting married, he'd asked 'Who to?'

A number of Sixty Somethings also thought the younger generations were more measured than they'd been and less prone to excesses. They are far more sensible than her generation, commented Charlotte. Alcohol was one area in question. Alison, for instance, said her children drink in different ways. They go for days not drinking at all and then have a good night out, drink huge amounts and feel terrible the next day. 'They are terribly abstemious on a Sunday evening,' she added. Carol thought there was a bit of a move towards being slightly disapproving of her generation and their lifestyles, and thinking more about their health, perhaps as a reaction to the previous generation's excesses. Being more measured extended into other areas of their lives. One woman thought younger people were less challenging than they'd been, that they were less politically active and less likely to protest against things they disliked. Her own daughter wouldn't go on strike because she was worried about the consequences and the effect on her promotion. Barbara agreed that students nowadays are less politically active than they were, and Sarah's explanation was that young people now have many more practical issues to deal with. Some women implied that there could also be an air of complacency. Younger people seem to think there's no need for women's rights and feminism now, said Hannah, that it's all okay now. 'But it isn't,' she said.

Whatever else they thought, the vast majority of the Sixty Somethings talked about being close to their children, and closer than they'd been to their own parents. Modern technology, and the ability to communicate on a regular basis, has certainly helped. But there was also a greater similarity in outlook across the generations which made communication easier and more informal. Children were dependent on their parents for longer, both emotionally and economically, and each were involved in each other's lives. 'What they want and we wanted out of life is pretty similar,' said Minnie. Norah agreed, adding that she thought they were as idealistic as they were. She said that when her daughter had gone to university she'd made a comment about changing the world. When her mother had laughed she'd got cross and retorted, 'The difference is you thought it, we're going to do it.'

Endnote

In the autumn of their lives, and with the benefit of experience and hindsight, would the Sixty Somethings go through it all again? And what advice would they give to younger people as they grow into older age?

Only about half as many women said they'd do it all again as said they wouldn't. Some of these would do everything exactly as before. 'Oh, what a nice idea,' said Elizabeth. 'I would love to do it all again. I don't think I'd do anything differently. I'd have my children again. I'd definitely do that again. It was definitely the best time. Planning everything in front of you. Planning the next one. Lovely.' Bella was in agreement, saying she would like her life over again 'not because I have regrets but because I've had such a nice time'. And Jacca's response was 'Yes, absolutely. I wouldn't have missed it for the world.' Others would like to have similar opportunities again, but might respond to them a bit differently. Helen, for example, would want to be more confident and make more decisions for herself, Norah would like to return with the knowledge she now had so that she avoided any little mistakes she'd made, and Ruby would want to get going on the work she now did from an earlier age. As Sarah said, 'hindsight is such a wonderful thing.' She had not been disappointed with her life, but 'the chance to tweak here and there would be good'. Primrose would like to have her life again and make more impact on the world.

There were a few women who might like to have their lives again, given certain provisos. Alice, for instance, would want a guarantee that her children would be more or less the same, while for several others it would depend on whether they could go back with the knowledge they'd gained over the years, and with greater confidence. For Carol, the decision would depend on having the opportunity to do certain things differently.

The majority of the women, however, were clear that once was enough. About a quarter of the total group said they would almost certainly not want to do it again and did not elaborate further. Others provided more of an explanation, pointing to the painful things they would have to go through again, the relief of not having to live through what the world was becoming, or the possibility that they might make even worse mistakes second time around. Verity did add, however, that she 'wouldn't mind going back to the sixties. I do remember them by the way. We had such fun.'

Drawing on their own experiences, their triumphs and their regrets, most women had some suggestions for younger people growing older. Not everyone, however, felt qualified to give advice, saying that people just have to work things out for themselves and make their own mistakes. that it was arrogant to tell others what to do, or that young people wouldn't listen anyway. Maureen quoted Maggie Smith as saying 'I don't give advice, I give opinions'.

Advice was nonetheless forthcoming, and ten central points emerged from what the women said. These were, in no particular order:

Don't worry
Try new things and be brave
Enjoy yourself
Understand yourself
Think of others
Communicate well

Save your money
Keep healthy
Maintain a good work-life balance
Keep important things in view

The importance of not worrying and being proactive in dealing with difficult issues was commonly stressed. 'Don't sweat the small stuff' was how Meg put it. This fed into being brave and not fearful of doing what had to be done. It was about having confidence, standing up for oneself and loved ones, trying new things and living each day 'as if it's your last'. Words such as 'adventurous' and 'independent' were mentioned, as were calls to spread one's wings and not follow like a sheep. In the words of Theresa, 'Try and do anything you want to do. If you don't do it, don't regret it. It's about not looking back and feeling sorry.' The clear message was 'just go for it'.

Enjoyment was valued too, and linked into grabbing opportunities as they arose. 'Follow your dreams and enjoy yourself and have fun,' said Miranda. Accept that growing old happens and do it as positively as you can, added another. Life's not very long, it was suggested, so 'just enjoy the entire ride'.

A good dose of self-belief was also seen as helpful. 'Think about yourself and decide how you want to move forward,' suggested Minnie, and trust your instincts. Understand about the seven ages of man, said Stephanie, know which one you're in and appreciate it. Don't shy away from self-examination, be true to yourself, accept yourself as you are and don't let anyone boss you around, were other comments. Be philosophical about anything that happens to you and learn from it. In Jane's words, 'it would be a wasted journey, this life, if you had the same opinions as you had when you were 18.' Hayley added that if you go through the motions of being happy, your emotions will eventually catch up with you. She'd started paying compliments twice a week to random strangers.

Thinking about other people, being kind and honest to them whatever their age and keeping friends were common recommendations. 'Remember that you are a human being and not a human doing,' said Mary. Optimal social interactions hung on good communication. Enjoy being with people and put down your screens was one piece of advice. And 'find out who others are and make space for them', was another. Think about how what you do affects other people including a partner, said Sarah, adding the advice to 'have a chat with the person you're retiring with' *before* you retire.

Many women advised younger people to save. Liza pointed out that it's nonsense to think that you will be happy if you are poor. It's never too early to plan for the future and get a pension sorted out, even if seems boring at the time. Helen added the recommendation to 'try not to get divorced', as that could be a massive disruption to finances. 'Go for the beta and not the alpha males,' said Hazel Grace, as 'they are likely to make you happier'. This, of course, was not everyone's sentiment.

Keeping healthy was central to the lives of many of the Sixty Somethings themselves, and regarded as essential for younger people too. The importance of eating well, staying fit, not abusing one's body and keeping an active brain were all mentioned.

Looking after oneself extended beyond diet and exercise and included getting a correct work-life balance and keeping some space for oneself. 'Nobody tends to say on their deathbed, I wish I'd spent more time in the office,' remarked Alice. This meant keeping the important things in view. Bear that in mind over your whole life, because if you rush around filling your life up with doing things all the time, you won't have time to find out who you yourself actually are. 'Every day is really really special,' said Winifred, 'so never ever ever give up. You might as well keep trying. Hope is the best thing in the world.'